Dedicated to my daughter Elsie, for teaching
me what it truly means to experience
and live in joy.

And to Leo, my son, for reminding me that
miracles can happen, even when you've
lost all hope.

*May you both always know that you are <u>more</u> than
good enough. I love you xx*

Contents

Introduction

Ever since I was a young girl, all I've ever wanted to do is write, and for my words to have the power to change the world.

No mean feat.

I'm Katie Portman, and as I'm putting pen to paper, I'm thirty-nine years old.

Some of you lovely readers may already know of me; if that's the case, feel free to move on and get cracking with the first chapter. For those that don't, though, I should tell you a little bit about myself. And, more importantly, how I came to write this book.

Seven years ago, I was pregnant with my first child— my daughter, Elsie—and it was then that I set up my blog: **Pouting In Heels**. I'd already been freelancing for a while, sharing my experiences of being self-employed, when I had the urge to set up a new, collaborative space where I could write about women's issues—in particular, the many challenges we so often face.

I had a deep desire to share my experiences, and to see if other women could relate to them. And so, my blog was born. It remains one of the best decisions I have ever made.

I had no idea then, in the early days of 2012, just how much the blog would change my life (and me) for the better.

Today, I'm thrilled to say that, despite the occasional hiccup or unforeseen challenge, Pouting In Heels is still going strong.

The blog has won awards, taken me to fabulous places, introduced me to many new friends, enabled me to work with household names, and pushed me out of my comfort zone on more than one occasion. It's also my main source of income.

But that isn't why I continue to do what I do.

Quite simply, I'd write even if it didn't earn me a single penny. I'd write even if few people read my words.

Like my love for dresses, red wine and books, writing is a huge part of what makes me…well, me! It's as essential to my survival as the air I breathe. I would be lost without it.

You'd perhaps think that after so many years writing about everything from motherhood to fashion, I'd find myself running out of things to say by now. I have been worried about this myself from time to time, too! Yet, here I am, very much an eager beaver, ready and raring to go.

There's just *so* much I still feel compelled to say about our lives as women today, in this complex, fast-moving, ever-changing world we inhabit.

About the many things we're afraid of, about the many things we love, and about the many difficult challenges we often face. Through my blog, I like to discuss the things that I believe hold us back or prevent us from being happier, content, or more successful in our lives.

In particular, I'm desperate to tackle the very thing I believe prevents us all from being our best selves or from living our best lives—the mistaken belief **that we are somehow not good enough.**

I believe women are continually fed this message throughout their lives, from the innocent days of childhood, to full-on, responsible adulthood.

And what's more, this message is *everywhere.*

Written in bold fonts across the front of the newspapers and magazines we read. Coming at us from our TV screens. Staring at us from heavily-airbrushed images.

Look around you, pay attention, and you will see that this message surrounds us.

Just the other day I was stood on my local train station platform with Elsie when I spotted an advert for a nearby shopping centre. Their message of enticement? They had everything I needed for a *'brand new me'*.

A few years ago, I wouldn't have even noticed this type of advertisement, but now I do—and it makes my blood boil.

'A brand new me'…what does this say to us all?

That **we are not, indeed *never,* good enough.** (Unless, of course, we do as the retailer wishes and spend money, possibly that which we can't afford, on clothes that we probably don't need, just to make us feel 'brand new'.)

These messages are dropped so subtly into our daily lives that most of us have become oblivious to it.

Why?

Because being told we're somehow not good enough has **become the norm**. This has got to stop.

I've spent most of my adult life trying to undo the damage this message has caused. And if I was a betting woman, I'd put money on it, that at some point during *your* life, you'll have accepted this ridiculously awful and toxic message in some form, too.

Perhaps you don't think you're slim enough, or successful enough, or pretty enough.

Maybe you fear you're not good enough to do the job you dream of.

Perhaps you believe you're just not good enough as a mother, daughter or friend.

Make no mistake, learning to trust that I **am good enough**, has been the biggest personal challenge of my life, and has put more obstacles in my path than anything else I can think of. *All* of my past difficulties have stemmed from an incorrect personal belief that in some way, shape, or form, I haven't been good enough.

So, I write about it.

Mainly for myself, but also in the hope that my thoughts may just help someone else slay their own inner demons.

To be clear, I am no expert, trained psychologist or guru. However, I am a woman who has turned her life around.

I've sat in the darkness and faced the bleakest, most terrifying bits of myself when I've had no choice but to do anything but. I've continually searched for glimmers of light in every god-awful situation, and worked hard to move myself towards a happier, more peaceful and content place, day after day after day.

Self-loathing? *Tick.*

Failures? *Tick.*

Feeling totally and utterly lost? You can tick a box for me on that one, too.

I've been there.

My psychology A-level teacher, who was incredibly wise and brilliant, once said to my mum when I got in a spot of bother at sixth-form college, 'You don't really need to worry about Katie, she's a survivor. Somehow, she'll always come out of things okay.'

And she was right. I always have.

Somehow, I've always managed to crawl my way out of whatever personal hellhole I've walked into, blindly or otherwise. But I like to think that I've done better than that.

Surviving, whilst necessary, is one thing, but thriving is another—and today, *this* is what I'm aiming for.

Digging myself out of holes is no longer enough. Today, I prefer to strut over them or avoid them altogether. I think people call that progress.

Our lives as modern women are full to the brim, overflowing with responsibilities and opportunities. Women have *so* much to offer the world yet, sadly, can often give away far too much of themselves for far too little.

I believe it's time we demanded more for ourselves, and for our sex. It doesn't matter what kind of life you live, we're *all* in a similar boat.

Whether you're a single woman who's busy smashing her career, or an exhausted stay-at-home mum to three young children under five, I know without even *knowing* you, that your life—like mine—will be full to the brim.

But how much of it truly makes us happy, and how much baggage could we drop to help lighten the incredible load we carry around?

This is the question I'm always thinking of as I try to figure things out in my own full yet admittedly-blessed life.

As a mum to two young children, and with a demanding career and business I love, my 'struggle with the juggle' is real and ongoing. But whilst my life is often chaotic, my peace of mind is slowly growing.

Many days I believe I have all the answers. Other days, like today, I feel like I have absolutely none.

At thirty-nine years of age, I have found my voice. More and more, I'm stepping up to claim my rightful place in the world.

Surviving. Shrinking. Keeping quiet. Playing things small… These things are no longer good enough for me. Sorry!

Am I flawed? You bet!

Have I much to learn? More than I can even begin to imagine.

Despite this, I've made considerable progress over the past two decades. I've doggedly chipped away at stale beliefs that did nothing but cause me misery.

I have instead accepted one very simple but revolutionary new belief.

I AM good enough. (And so, for the record, **are YOU**.)

I have *so* many wishes for this book. Ultimately, I hope that it will 'speak' to you and inspire you to think differently about who you are and who you are destined to become.

I hope that within these pages you discover that you're never alone in how you think or feel.

I hope that you will finish it feeling more empowered.

I hope that it will encourage you to look at yourself—and other women—through much kinder and more-accepting eyes.

More than anything, I hope that it will help you realise that **you are imperfectly perfect just as you are.**

There really is no need, as that billboard exclaimed, for a 'brand new you'. In my experience, to live a happier and more successful life, you must learn to love and accept the old one.

And so, if this book and my words can somehow get you started on that kinder self-love journey, I will die a very happy woman indeed.

Thank you for allowing me to share my thoughts and words with you.

Now, let's start a revolution!

JEALOUSY

Jealousy

*'Learning to not envy someone else's blessings is
what grace looks like.'*

~ Rupi Kaur

At ten years-old I was taken over by the green-eyed monster. For the first time in my life, I longed to be someone else.

I wanted to be the new girl at school.

The girl with the unbelievably shiny hair that swung perfectly, side to side, as she walked through the playground with all the grace of a seasoned supermodel walking the catwalk.

She was perfect.

I'd steal glances at her and marvel at her cool get-ups that set her apart from the rest of us. She wore ra-ra skirts with sneakers, and I thought she was the most magnificent girl I'd ever known. I absolutely idolised her, and forever longed to be part of her inner circle.

My jealousy, however, prevented us from ever becoming good friends.

Whenever I was in her presence, I never felt good about myself. Unsurprisingly, I didn't like this very much, so I kept a safe and chilly distance from the girl with the perfect hair.

At that age, I didn't really understand why I was jealous of someone I adored so much. But now, as a grown woman, I totally get it.

It was the mistaken belief that, because her light shone so brightly, mine had to dim.

It was the mistaken belief that I wasn't as special, talented, or as beautiful as her.

It was the mistaken belief that being near her somehow made me 'less than'.

Back then, I decided that it was better to admire her from afar than ever risk her light outshining my own.

I've learned to accept the green-eyed monster that sometimes stomps into my psyche and makes herself at home.

It's true that I don't like her very much. She makes far too much noise that drowns out my rational thinking, for starters, and if I'm not careful, she makes me behave in all manner of incredibly foolish ways.

But, somehow, I've come to accept her. I guess you could even say we're friends.

She isn't so bad, that green-eyed monster. Not if you look her directly in the eyes. Head on.

And not if you ask her, 'What the hell's going on here then?!'

As monstrous as her presence can feel, I've learned that jealousy can actually be a marvellous unraveller of the truth. Let me give you an example. As a blogger, one of the best bits about my admittedly-bonkers career is that I cross paths with other bloggers from all walks of life. Over the years, I've met a number of bloggers who have become rather famous (deservedly so). Their numbers are shooting up fast on social media. Their faces are used for national advertising campaigns, and they're earning money that was probably once beyond their wildest dreams.

I'm happy for them. Genuinely.

But…here comes the truth. Often, when I hear of their successes, jealousy can hit me like a sledgehammer.

Bloggers, in case you're not aware, are reliant on

self-promotion. It therefore becomes near-impossible to escape other people's success when you work within the online world as I do.

Enter the green-eyed monster.

Instead of allowing her to take up permanent residence, however, I prefer to block her at the front door and ask her some questions instead.

I look her square in the eye and say something along the lines of, 'Okay then, missy. What's going on here? Just why *are* you showing up here again?'

I've found that if I don't let fear get to me (because, confronting any monster is pretty scary, after all) she will soon come back to me with an answer that goes a little like this: 'You're feeling jealous because you want what they have. You're feeling jealous because you wish that had happened to you. You're feeling jealous because you mistakenly think that because they have it, you never will.'

Uncovering some perhaps painful home truths is good, and definitely preferable to being consumed by jealousy. However, I've also learned that these answers are not enough.

They're a great place to start, don't get me wrong, but to *really* benefit from the green-eyed monster's loud presence—to *really* put her to work—I find I have to pick her answers apart at the seams and do my best to unravel what they really mean.

Here's an example of the kind of inner dialogue I try to have with myself when jealousy pops up to say hello: 'Okay, so if I want what they have, what can I do about it?

'Well, I guess I could learn from them. I could take a closer look at their success and figure out what they're doing that I'm not.

'And I guess I should be thankful to them, too. Because

if I want something they have, that's **the best indicator** of what I want to achieve and do with my life.'

Jealousy is horrible when it knocks you off your feet. It can destroy everything good that you've created and make you feel like you're never good enough (notice how this keeps popping up?).

Or…we can try and take something positive from it. It's not easy, and it often goes against what we think we want to do, which is stay in our festering pit of envy, but if we accept and allow the monster in and allow her to speak, jealousy can provide us with useful answers.

Jealousy happens. However, we can choose to deal with it in a healthier and more positive way.

When it comes to experiencing jealousy, we are *never* alone.

This is something else I've learned over the past decade or so, and something that occasionally I find surprising. Everyone experiences it. Even—take a second to let this sink in—the **very people you envy**, who seem to 'have it all'. And that's okay. Good, even!

We've all met someone who makes us feel inadequate. We've all suffered from the fear of being outshone. It's human nature; we're as fragile as we are robust. No one is immune to envy or their self-confidence plummeting. The only difference is that wiser people make a conscious effort to *not* allow the jealousy to destroy them.

The woman you envy from afar will, I guarantee, have had her fair share of green-eyed monsters rearing their ugly heads.

But if she believes she's enough, it will not have the same impact that it does on those who don't believe this. Sure, she'll feel it when jealousy hits her, but if she knows her own worth, she'll learn from it and soon manage to shake it off. It won't dent her self-esteem, nor will it prevent her from doing anything. In fact, if she truly likes herself, she'll use what jealousy is trying to teach her to grow, prosper and move the hell on.

People who like themselves not only experience jealously less, they also deal with it better when it takes hold.

They know it's normal and, crucially, they understand that their light will always remain strong, even when they feel like they're being outshone.

They appreciate that, in life, there are times when somebody's light **is meant to shine brighter than others** and understand that we all get a chance to have our moment in the spotlight.

They know that being around a woman whose light shines brightly doesn't have to make them feel bad, and that it can—if we allow it—even help our own light to shine a little brighter, too.

They realise that the green-eyed monster will destroy them and shatter their self-worth if they ignore her messages and give her room to move in.

So, as well as accepting what we're feeling and asking some tricky questions, what else should we do when jealousy punches us in the guts out of nowhere?

There are a number of tactics I've used over the years that always help me out whenever the green-eyed monster appears.

Firstly, as I've mentioned already, you need to identify where it's coming from and why it's making you feel the way it does.

Finding the source of the jealousy is the key, because that's when you can pick it apart and figure out what on earth is going on.

Say, for instance, it's always one particular person that causes you to have a surge in jealousy. In this scenario, I find I have two choices: one, I can limit contact with that person until I'm in a better place. Two, I can choose to humanise the person.

If jealousy enters my psyche when I'm scrolling through Instagram and come across a particular person, I can choose to **stop** following them.

Admittedly, social media comes with its own ginormous bag of problems (enough to fill another book), but, if someone is continually making you feel inadequate or insecure—intentionally or otherwise—limit or, in some cases, remove contact where possible.

As for the humanising bit, this is the thing I find works wonders. From my experience, jealousy tends to take root and bloom **when I believe a person to be better than I am or that they have a better life than me.**

It's possible to fix this by making a conscious effort to see the person through kinder, and more realistic, eyes. Next time you meet a person that makes you feel insanely jealous, **make them more human.**

A person may seem to 'have it all' or appear to be the most stylish or self-assured woman in the room, but you have absolutely no idea what's going on in their lives or in their heads.

Take them off the mental pedestal you've put them on and remind yourself that no one on this planet is perfect.

Remind yourself that everyone—including this person—is dealing with struggles and challenges on a daily basis that others aren't aware of.

Remember, when you meet or get to know someone, what you're seeing **is just a tiny glimpse of their life.**

Remember: you are good enough, and so are they.

If you can and want to go one step further, I recommend trying to get to know people better. Be pleasant, strike up a conversation and connect. The more we get to know someone, the harder it is to be jealous of them, because we begin to see them as rounded, flawed individuals instead of someone who appears to have, or be, everything we've ever desired.

Let the people who unknowingly feed your green-eyed monster **teach and inspire you.**

If you're jealous of a school mum who always looks stylish and pulled together, look at ways in which you can improve your own physical image.

If you're jealous of a woman you work with who is always being promoted ahead of you, try to learn what she does differently—or, better still, ask her for some advice.

Above all, remember, in most cases, the person we're jealous of does not intentionally create those feelings within us.

We do.

Think of the person you envy as a mirror that can show you all the insecurities you bury, or all the dreams and desires you've yet to fulfil.

When you think about them in this way, you could even argue that they're a blessing.

§

Be grateful.

We're often told this as a child. *Be grateful for your Christmas presents. Be grateful that you have a roof over your head and food to eat, etc.* I think most of us have had this message drilled into us at a young age.

And yet, for some bizarre reason, gratitude can be easily overlooked and, at worst, totally forgotten.

In the western world we live in a society that preys on our insecurities, insidiously whispering in our ears that we lack things. **That we're not enough**.

'Lack' is *the* perfect breeding ground for jealousy; thankfully, gratitude is the perfect antidote.

Certainly, it appears to be for me. Over the past twelve months I've tried to exercise gratitude and have created a routine of expressing thanks on an (almost) daily basis. After reading many books about the life-changing impact of gratitude, I thought I'd give it a go. To my own astonishment, it's had a *huge* impact.

I can't deny that when I first started rolling off lists of thanks, it felt a little weird. On at least one occasion I caught myself rolling my eyes. Often, it felt silly. Sometimes, it felt pathetic and, for all my spiritual leanings, there were times when it felt a bit 'woo-woo', even for me.

Then, things started to happen, and I soon realised that, actually, the gratitude business isn't silly.

After a few days I noticed that I felt happier. I realised that, as time went on, I was becoming less critical of myself and less critical of others, too.

I began to see things differently. I knew it was working when I walked into a room my kids had quickly turned into a bombsite with their toys, and instead of feeling annoyed or exasperated by the mess like I usually would have, I actually felt thankful.

Granted, the mess didn't look good, but it was a reminder of how very blessed I've been, twice over, to be a mum, and that my children know how to play.

There's a lot to be said for counting our blessings. Besides my initial doubts, I have found that being truly grateful for things is a game-changer where life and emotional heath is concerned.

That's all well and good, I hear you cry, but how does that relate to jealousy?

Quite a lot, actually. Whereas gratitude comes from a place of appreciation and thankfulness, jealousy comes from a place of *lack*. The belief that there isn't enough to go around, and that if someone else has something, you can't have it.

The belief that whatever you do isn't good enough. The belief that *you* are not good enough, and that you will never be good enough until you buy that detached house, drive a silver Ferrari, or lose twenty pounds, for example.

Lack is the root cause of our jealousy, which is why gratitude saves the day.

If you constantly feel like you're not enough, or that what you *have* is not enough, take a closer look around you. Find things to be grateful for and say '**thank you**'.

Do it as much as you possibly can—every day, ideally—but especially when the green-eyed monster raises her ugly head.

I like to do my 'gratitude thing' late at night, just as my head hits the pillow, and whilst the house is nice and quiet. Sometimes, if I've had a bad day, it can be a struggle to conjure up more than a couple of things. Other days, my checklist of thanks can go on and on.

I occasionally forget to do it, or I'll fall asleep as I'm rattling through my list. On the days I do remember to do it, I *always* find it helps. There's no doubt in my mind that what we focus on, grows. Our minds are *very* fertile.

If I focus on lack and not having enough, this is what comes back to me—multiplied!

But, if I switch things around and make a real effort to be grateful, more good things seem to come my way.

Replace '*woe is me*' with '*wow is me!*' and watch your life improve.

It's difficult to be jealous of others when you know just how much you have to be thankful for yourself.

I want to talk about one more thing to do with jealousy—something you may never have thought of.

Have you ever stopped to think that people may be jealous of you?

I say this because we're often so wrapped up in our own misery or feelings towards other people that we forget others may be looking at us and our lives and feeling that suffocating fog of jealousy, too.

It's easy to forget that what we feel, other people feel, too. As I've said before, you are never alone, even when it comes to the green-eyed monster.

Maybe, for example, whilst you're trying to control feelings of jealousy surging through your body when you come across the woman in the office that seems to have it all…guess what? There could very well be another woman there who's looking at you in exactly the same way.

We've all felt that longing to hop out of our own lives and into someone else's. We've all felt that desire to swap our trusty comfortable shoes for someone else's more glamorous or alluring pair.

§

Have you ever complimented someone and seen a look of astonishment flash across their face? Or noticed how someone will respond to a compliment by quickly pointing out a self-perceived fault or flaw? Women can be *so* hard on themselves; we can be *so* critical of who we are. Many of us struggle to accept a simple, gracious compliment.

Many of us won't dare to believe it. We're so unkind to ourselves.

Instead of focusing on what we *do* have and what we *can* offer, we turn our self-hatred towards other women and let jealousy consume us.

We've all done it. I'll hold my hand up here; there have been plenty of times in my life when I've been jealous of another woman crossing my path.

As I've mentioned, there was the new girl at school; and, through no fault of their own, there have been many other females who have unwittingly brought my insecurities to the surface and made me feel dreadfully inadequate.

Yet, just as I've been jealous of others, I've also been aware over the years that, on occasion, other women have been jealous of *me*.

Beneath the hurt and feelings of lack that we inevitably experience at points in our lives, **we're essentially all the same.**

The green-eyed monster never discriminates. She pops up within all of us from time to time, especially when we feel threatened, inadequate, or in any way 'less than'. Her presence is not the nicest, but if we do our best to understand that she's more common than we perhaps first thought and give her the chance to speak to us and reflect back the areas of ourselves/our lives that need work, she can be an easy monster to tame and a very good teacher.

'Pick Ups' to Take Away

♥ Jealousy can *and will* devour you, but only if you let it. Like all monsters, the green-eyed one has no power over you unless you give it to her.

♥ When jealousy hits: stop, acknowledge it, then take a few moments to ask yourself, *'What's going on here? Why am I feeling this way?'*

♥ Experiencing jealousy can be a blessing - it's all about how you choose to see it. It's not easy, but if you probe the green-eyed monster, you will find that she can provide you with powerful insight.

♥ If you can, figure out where your jealousy is coming from. Use this information to improve yourself and your life.

♥ When someone sparks jealousy in you, think: *distance* and/or *humanise*.

♥ Feelings of jealousy are created by *you* - no one else. Other people are merely mirrors that have the power to reflect your insecurities, and your unfulfilled dreams and desires.

♥ 'Lack' is the breeding ground for jealousy, but gratitude can stop it from growing.

♥ Kill the monster with thanks. Ditch the lack mentality. Stop focusing on what you *don't* think you have and start appreciating everything that you *do* have.

♥ Remember that *everyone* experiences jealousy from time to time; it's how you deal with it that counts. It's ridiculously common, more so than many of us realise, but it doesn't have to hold you back.

FEAR

Fear

'I think women are scared of feeling powerful and strong and brave sometimes. There's nothing wrong with being afraid. It's not the absence of fear, it's overcoming it; sometimes, you just have to blast through and have faith.'

~ Emma Watson

There are many things I fear in my life.

Some fears are serious - like my children getting ill or my loved ones dying; no doubt these are fears you'll share with me.

I'm going to let you into a secret and tell you that I'm often afraid of writing. What do you make of that?!

For as long as I can remember, the only thing I've ever wanted to do with my life is read and write. When I was a little girl, my mum would have to practically wrestle books out of my hands in the morning, so she could get me to school on time. At eight years-old, I made my own little magazines from scratch.

I've kept journals, written poems and entered short story competitions. I'm an English graduate and a trained journalist. I write for a living and I adore words, but yes, as irrational as it seems, I am often afraid to sit down and work with them. Or, to be more exact, to publish them.

As I sit here typing away, every so often stopping to take a sip of Yorkshire tea, I can feel familiar butterflies in my stomach dancing about as I do my best to weave cohesive sentences together.

Their presence is only slight, but mighty enough to make me aware that I'm working on something that really matters to me. That's when I can become more than a little scared.

As you'd rightly expect, this book matters a great deal to me. Not only is it the culmination of years of hard work, it's also a dream of mine realised. I've fantasised about writing a book for as long as I've been reading them.

Now the opportunity is here, whilst admittedly I'm excited and giddy with joy, there is a part of me that's truly terrified. You don't hear many people talking about the rising feeling of fear or anxiety that can occur when sitting down to write. There's a reason writers' block happens and why so many books or pieces of written work remain unfinished.

It's through fear.

As I write this book, I'm frightened that the words may not come—or that, when they do, they'll be the wrong ones.

I'm frightened that no one will read my words and that my efforts will have been in vain.

And I'm frightened that if people *do* read them, they'll hate what I've written, hate me for writing them, or worst still, won't feel anything at all.

'What will people think of me? Am I good enough to write a book? What if I can't finish it?! What if people hate it?!' These are the thoughts that repeatedly swirl around inside my head as I type. Never have I felt the fear of writing more acutely than sitting down to write this book.

I can imagine what you're thinking: why on earth am I doing something that makes me feel so nervous and fearful? Why start something that has the potential to cause me so much distress? To put it simply, because I have to.

If I was in any *real* doubt about whether or not I

should write this book, the presence of fear has made it a no-brainer. Because, when I feel fear, I choose to see it as a big green flashing light for **GO**.

Cast your mind back to all the times you've felt fearful in your life. Think about what was at stake. Success? Love? Happiness? Adventure? Safety, maybe?

When fear is present, I've found it's usually due to one of these things. (And, occasionally, because of a few other things, too.)

Maybe you felt fear at a job interview or when you took your driving test. Perhaps you felt it when you walked down the aisle to get married, or when standing in-front of a room full of people to deliver an important presentation.

Maybe you've felt fearful when calling the doctors to get test results, or when walking home late at night.

Fear can paralyse us if we allow it. Ultimately, its job is to keep us safe, to remind us what matters, and perhaps even liberate us.

I used to hate the sensation of fear. Like, *really* hated it. That nervous feeling, that strange fluttering in my tummy…I'd do anything to avoid it.

As a child, then as a teenager, the occasional presence of fear alarmed me and brought me great discomfort. Naturally, I'd try to make it disappear at all costs.

In school, if I knew the answer to a question, I'd think about raising my hand to let the teacher know I had something to say. At that point, an unsettling feeling would quickly descend on me and I'd keep my hand firmly on the desk instead.

Back then, I mistakenly believed fear vanished more quickly if you remained quiet, unseen and unchallenged. And, to some extent, I was right.

The thing I *didn't* realise, which I know all too well

now, is that fear is a funny old thing. Just when you think it's disappeared for good, it **comes back, harder and faster than before.**

The less I spoke up in class, the more frightened I became of even contemplating it. The less I challenged myself, the more frightened I was of even *thinking* about trying anything that fell outside of my comfort zone.

Fear, if we're not careful, can trick us into creating a prison for ourselves. The more we work at trying to block the feeling from arising, the higher our prison walls become.

Ignoring fear, or trying to prevent its presence, only fuels its momentum.

It does not—as I once wrongly believed—stop it in its tracks.

So, what does?

Like many of us, I've had endless battles with fear throughout my life, and after trying all manner of tactics to get rid of it or limit its impact, I've come to this conclusion: **the only way to truly tackle fear is to use it to your advantage.**

Is this easy? Hell, no. But, it can and must be done.

Attempting to block the presence of fear does not work at getting rid of it. Indeed, as I've just mentioned, more often than not it actually serves to bolden it. If you want to lessen the impact of personal fear, you must give it attention and respect. Which is why, these days, I like to think of the presence of fear as an effective personal indicator that tells me when a challenge is on its way. My very own alarm system, if you will.

Everything I've ever been afraid of doing in my life—from falling in love to writing this book, giving birth to taking my driving test—has been the making of me as a human being. And if you take a minute to think of the things you've been fearful of doing, too, you'll likely feel the same as me.

For example, standing in front of a couple of hundred people to do my first ever public presentation was the most terrifying prospect I could have imagined. Here's the crazy thing: once I actually got up there and my nerves eased, *I actually began to enjoy myself.*

My throat went dry, and it wasn't the most perfect delivery. I felt shaky and slightly nauseous when I was at the front, but every second of the struggle was worth it, because I came away from that presentation feeling like I'd climbed my own personal Everest. I felt on top of the world.

That challenge remains one of my proudest moments to date. Not because it was the best presentation the world has seen, but because I tackled a fear I'd *carried around with me for decades.*

Opportunities for me to speak in public had arisen before that day, but I'd been so fearful of even thinking about standing up in front of everyone that I never, ever took the baton. Instead, I carried around an invisible bag of fear on my shoulders emblazoned with *'too scared to speak in public!'*, which got heavier and more uncomfortable as the years went by.

Then one day, out of the blue, I received an email from a woman I greatly admire and respect, asking me to consider speaking at a local business event about the natural evolution of my career from journalist to blogger. My initial thought was, 'No bloody way!'

Of course, I had to respond, so I politely enquired about payment, expecting that I'd be told there was no money available or that it would only be a small amount—

both of which would give me the perfect excuse to bow out gracefully at the first hurdle and give my rising fear the elbow.

The universe, it seemed, had a different plan concerning my public speaking career. To my utter astonishment, the financial offer that came back was so impressive that it left me with little choice but to accept and say I'd do it. With butterflies whirling and dread descending, I agreed to do the presentation.

I felt proud of myself for finally deciding to give it a go, but it wasn't easy. I'm really not exaggerating in the slightest here when I say I worried about it for several months, or that, as time got nearer to the '*MOST FRIGHTENING DAY OF MY LIFE*', I began to panic.

This wasn't helped when I did some research about presentations and came across some startling statistics. Studies showed that more people are afraid of public speaking than death.

Human beings are more afraid of standing up in front of other humans and talking than we are about leaving this world, a statistic that didn't help my visions of disaster.

But, here's another important thing I've learned about fear: just when you think it's going to be the death of you, magic starts to happen. My magician arrived in the form of Lisa. A wise, warm, wonderful human-being who, rather incredibly, appeared in my life just when I needed her.

We met at one of her public speaking events and instantly got on like a house of fire. And after confiding in her about my utter terror of public speaking and my looming presentation, she gave me one of the simplest but greatest pieces of advice I've ever received: 'Think of nerves as excitement.'

She's a genius. That snippet of advice worked brilliantly for me.

It makes perfect sense when you think about it. The physical feelings we experience when we're frightened of something are the **same feelings we get when we're excited about something.**

The very things I've been most frightened of doing in my life—marriage, motherhood, self-employment, for example—have also been the things I've been most excited about, too.

Whilst physically, fear and excitement may be the same, the difference in how you perceive them both is *huge*!

So, I changed my mindset. I embraced the opportunity. I tried to enjoy it as much as possible, and when it came to the big day itself, I put my energy into owning the experience and giving it my all. I prepared for it; I constantly told myself that I was going to enjoy it, and I went for it.

My fear of public speaking lessened after that day. Astonishingly, the excitement for it remained and I now look forward to public speaking with relish.

Yes, me! The woman who, as a teenager, used to shrink into her chair rather than put her hand up in class and speak out, now loves to be at the front, on her own, speaking to a room full of strangers.

If someone from the future had told me this, I would never have believed it in a million years. This is what happens when you make the effort to tackle a fear.

You end up surprising yourself more than you ever thought possible, in the *very* best way.

I often wonder what would have happened if I'd turned down that opportunity. I wonder how much duller and restrictive my life and career would be.

Saying no was undoubtedly the easiest and safest option for me at that time in my life, yet something inside me paid attention to my inner voice that was repeatedly whispering 'yes'.

Whispering to me, cheering me on to have a go.

Whispering to me, urging me to tackle a fear that had held me within its grasp for so many years.

Whispering to me, 'Katie, what if…?!'

Because this is what fear and excitement both do, isn't it? Whisper 'what if…?!'

'*What if* I fall over in front of hundreds of people?'—FEAR

'*What if* I get this job and end up travelling the world?'—EXCITEMENT

'*What if* people laugh at my outfit?'—FEAR

'*What if* I fall pregnant and get to become a mother?'—EXCITEMENT (and, quite possibly, a bit of fear, too)

The only thing that separates fear from excitement is that one emotion questions your choices whilst the other dares to explore them.

Next time a 'what if?' whispers to you, listen carefully and choose how you respond. It doesn't take much to switch things round and swap fear for excitement.

§

It's true that the presence of fear doesn't feel good. At its worst, it can cause paralysis and prevent us from moving even the tiniest step forward.

I still believe it's a **great indicator**.

Fear raises a large red or white flag (depending on the nature of the situation), making it very clear that we need to act.

When I feel its presence and sense one of those flags rising, I know in an instant that I'm onto something.

If I don't act? Then I'll forever remain in stasis.

Fear is there to alarm us, warning us that our life may be in danger, for example. It's also there to challenge us and force us out of our comfortable, easy seat.

Whenever I feel fear, I 'do'. I'll hit the publish button on a blog post I've been terrified of writing, which often end up being the more popular articles with my readers.

I'll continue to write this book, even though I'm terrified you won't like it. Because if I don't, I'll regret it forever.

I'll try new things, even if I'm worried that I'll fail or look stupid. Why on Earth am I here if not to learn and grow?

That's what I've learned. That the best way to stop that awful feeling of fear paralysis—indeed, the only way—is **to take a leap of faith.**

You owe it to yourself to have a go at whatever it is that makes you fearful.

You owe it to your life to make the most of it, regardless of how terrifying something may seem.

Make the jump…and do it often. The more you leap towards the unknown, the easier it gets, and the less fear will be able to hold you in its paralysing grip.

Surround yourself with people that are good at leaping. Encourage your children to be leapers, too.

When you take a leap of faith, the universe tends to put its arms out to catch you. Your job—your only job—is to put the magic to the test and run and jump as high as you possibly can.

'Pick Ups' to Take Away

♥ Many of the things you are afraid of can, and will, be the making of you, if you *allow* them to be.

♥ Fear will not be the death of you (although it can often feel like it will be when the feelings emerge); however, it *will* shrink your life and paralyse you mentally if you don't tackle what it is that you're afraid of.

♥ **Ignoring fear or trying to prevent it only gives it more momentum**. It does not—as I once wrongly believed—stop it in its tracks.

♥ Physically, fear and excitement feel the same, but the difference mentally is *huge*! Where possible, learn to flip your mindset.

♥ Try to think of fear as nothing more than your personal alarm system and an indicator that you need to take some form of action as soon as possible.

♥ The best way to stop fear controlling you is to do the very thing you're afraid of and take a leap of faith.

♥ The more you attempt to tackle your fears, the easier it becomes.

♥ When you take a leap of faith, magic starts to happen. The universe will do its best to support you.

♥ Surround yourself with 'leapers', i.e. people that are great at tackling their fears.

GUILT

Guilt

'Women are their own worst enemies. And guilt is the main weapon of self torture…show me a woman who doesn't feel guilty and I'll show you a man.'

~ Erica Jong

Modern women are experts at feeling guilty.

Every woman I know seems to struggle with feelings of guilt, and I am no exception.

Just this morning, I felt guilty because my daughter wanted me to go outside and play with her in the sunshine, but I couldn't, because I had work to do.

Yesterday, I felt guilty because I almost forgot a friend's birthday, and just a few days prior I felt guilty because I ate too much chocolate cake.

I feel it *all* the time.

From motherhood guilt that can sometimes feel overwhelming in its intensity, to lesser pangs of guilt that pop up continually, this emotion is one I struggle with on a daily basis. And I know I'm not alone.

We all seem to struggle with the guilt load. You only have to glance at social media to see women sharing their 'I feel bad because…' stories. Crack open a bottle of wine with your closest friends and you'll soon find that we're masters at beating ourselves up for not being, or doing, better.

Female guilt has become our Achilles' heel, and as our lives become busier and increasingly challenging, it's becoming more painful to bear.

So, where does this guilt come from?

I have a few theories about this, but first I'd like you to think back to your childhood days and carefully consider the messages you were no doubt given.

As a young Katie, I was told many wonderful things, most of which has stood me in good stead over the years and helped me to grow and develop from a girl to a teen, then into a woman.

There are two key messages I've heard repeatedly throughout my life, which now, as an adult, I'm not too fond of.

Be nice.

Look pretty.

From an early age, most young girls are taught that it's incredibly important to 'be nice' and 'look pretty'.

We receive these messages, which are seemingly harmless, from everywhere—from our loved ones to our friends, from peers to wider society.

How many times as a young girl did you hear someone compliment you on how pretty you were, or how nice your dress was?

Or—and this might be painful to admit, and even I hold my hands up to this one—how many times have you, as an adult woman, complimented a girl only on how she looks or how nice she has been?

On the surface, there's nothing wrong with these messages. After all, it *is* nice to be nice, and it's rather lovely to look pretty, too.

It becomes a problem when these are the *only* things we're complimented on or judged by, just because we happen to be female.

I ask you, when was the last time you saw or heard a male politician being judged on his attire or asked about his shoes? Yet this is the reality female politicians face every single day.

Be truthful and ask yourself: how many times have *you* complimented a girl or another woman on her talent, courage, humour or leadership, instead of her new dress, weight loss or change of hairstyle?

The 'be nice and look pretty' message has skewed our thinking. It's become so engrained in us, so much a part of our female identity, that we're not even aware we're failing to appreciate other women for who they are or what they offer. Worst still, we even apply this same attitude towards our daughters.

And what happens when you don't feel like you've met the high standards today's women are judged by? *You feel bad.*

We berate ourselves for not being good enough and head down the well-heeled path of guilt that has been painfully carved out by generations of women who have walked before us.

Be nice. Look nice. Two little messages that have shackled us for all eternity.

They are why we feel bad if we tell catcallers to get knotted when they blatantly harass us as we walk down the street.

They are why we find ourselves occasionally apologising for our appearance when we feel embarrassed or shameful about how we look.

They are why we often ignore our gut instincts about a man who makes us feel unsafe or uncomfortable.

They are why we feel bad when we believe we've eaten too much.

They are why we don't ask for the pay rises we know we deserve.

Be nice and look nice. Or feel horrendously guilty if you don't.

§

Most of us experience guilt. It is, of course, a natural reaction if we're in the wrong, if we've hurt someone, or we've done something we're ashamed of.

Feeling guilt is part and parcel of being a decent human being, and in many ways, essential to our moral development.

Women, however, also tend to feel bad about things they really ***shouldn't*** feel guilty about. Take, for instance, being a mum. Never has guilt had such a hold on me than when I became a mother. The moment that plastic stick displayed 'pregnant' on its tiny digital screen, motherhood guilt stuck to me like a limpet. From giving birth to how I fed my baby. From decisions over their sleeping routine to how I tackled any undesirable behaviour.

When you're a mum, parental guilt follows you around; it's almost impossible to shake. And when you throw any semblance of a career into the motherhood mix, you can ramp your guilt levels up a hundred times over.

I don't think I've met a mum yet who doesn't feel guilty at some point about her work/life balance—about working too much, too little, or not at all.

The media often likes to put mums in camps and pit us against each other, as they argue the toss about whose work or parenting choices are right or wrong. It doesn't really matter who they crown the winner; *all* women are made to feel guilty for how they live their lives and parent their children.

We feel guilty for the choices we make, even though

they're made with the best intentions. When this guilt consumes us and makes us feel truly awful we fall into the trap set by the media and condemn choices made by other mums, in a bid to make ourselves feel better.

Does this sound familiar? *'My parenting choices may not be perfect, but they're better than how so and so does things...'*

And on it goes.

We're made to feel guilty, so we do.

I continually feel like I'm failing to pin down the perfect work/life balance. I work from home, which comes with its own set of challenges; I work for myself, which is wonderful, but not easy when you have small children around.

I've been complimented on how I manage things and also been told that my lifestyle is enviable, yet these comments fall on deaf ears, because I *always* feel guilty about working too much or not working enough. Even though **I know better**.

Like all of us, I like to think I try my best. I work hard. I make decisions that I believe are right for myself and my family. Still the guilt comes and steals my sleep; I'm often lying awake at 3 a.m. in the morning, ruminating over what I could have done differently or better.

We've been sold a lie. A big fat whopper of a lie sold to us as a dream.

It sounded wonderful. It promised so much. But, far from being empowering, it haunts and taunts us in equal measure.

'Women can have it ALL...'

'We can have it ALL?!'

A few simple words that increase the pressure and guilt women already feel.

Having it all isn't possible (or, at least, not all at once).

It never has been possible, and it never will be possible. It's time we accepted this.

If you find that depressing, I can understand that. But my goal isn't to make you feel bad—quite the contrary. **It's to make you feel better.**

A beautiful family. A wonderful career. A perfect marriage. A killer wardrobe. Pots of money. A jet-set lifestyle. Enviable success. A size ten figure.

Of course I want all of that—who wouldn't?!

But after trying to obtain all these things all at once—and finding myself succeeding in one area but failing in many others—I soon realised that this statement, whilst wonderfully aspirational, **is far from empowering in reality.**

On the surface, 'we can have it all!' dangles possibilities and fuels hope, but dig a little deeper and what you'll find isn't *potential* but *pressure*. And masses and masses of guilt.

I've tried bloody hard to have it all, but it's impossible.

Does that make me a failure? No. Does that mean I'm not happy? Absolutely not. It does make me feel guilty from time to time, though, and it does make me feel like I'm not doing enough.

You may feel guilty when you leave the office at the end of the day, because you believe that you should invest more time in your work and career (even though you have other commitments and you're already exhausted).

You may believe that when your child has a typical toddler tantrum at nursery, that it's your fault because you should spend more quality time with them (even though you already give your child as much quality time as you possibly can).

You might beat yourself up because you believe the reason you're not slimmer is because you're not strict enough with what you eat (even though you barely get five minutes to yourself each day to eat *anything*).

'Women can have it all!' This is what we're told. This is what we see. This is what we hear. And on we go, trying even harder, working even longer and pushing ourselves even more.

The dream still out of reach, we end up feeling stressed and demoralised, and compare our lives unfavourably to others (others that may seem to have it all; however, I promise you that, behind closed doors, no one really does). We become stuck in a cycle of frustration.

If we could only find out what it is we're doing wrong. How come our lives don't thrive the way we're told they should when we work so hard?

Have you ever noticed that it's relatively easy to make one area of your life a success when you focus your time and energy on it? Do you find, though, that as soon as you get one aspect of your life on track one or two of the other elements go completely to pot?

Perhaps you're great at ticking things off your to-do list. But, do you ever actually finish that damn list, or does it just get bigger every day?

This is normal.

Life, as a wise person once said, isn't about the destination but the journey.

Whilst we should strive to identify areas we can improve, we should also understand that we will never get everything done. That we will never be perfect in every area of our lives, or in every single thing we do.

We just can't.

It's terribly sad that we're sold the idea that we *can* have everything; all it does is leave us feeling perpetually guilty for not managing to achieve the impossible.

Why can't I have it all? What am I doing wrong?'

Guilt blooms when we mistakenly believe we're letting ourselves down or not trying hard enough. Here's a radical thought: **let that statement go.**

Get off the guilt wagon you've ridden for so long and give your tired, heavily-burdened shoulders a break.

Occasionally, in my career, I'm interviewed for a website or magazine. This is a common question I'm asked: 'Is it possible for women to have it all?'

I always reply, '**Yes, I believe it can be possible, just not all at once.**'

This is what I tell myself. This is what I aim for. A life that's full to the brim, but *not* one that's perfect. A life that offers possibilities and fulfilment in different areas at different times, but *not* one in which I feel pressured to achieve everything, every day.

When I brought my newborn daughter home for the first time, I was determined to be the most committed, loving, hands-on mum I could be. I'd longed for my baby for so many years, and to finally have her home with me— my beautiful, healthy bundle of joy—meant *everything.*

I gave her my all and I loved it.

After a few weeks I began to notice that, whilst I was seemingly flourishing in my new role as a mum, other aspects of my life were not quite as rosy. The house was untidy, and it hadn't been cleaned in weeks. The washing and ironing piles grew bigger by the day.

Physically, I didn't look my best, and exhaustion began to set in. My husband and I began to snap at each other, and we rowed over stupid things because we were shattered. I hadn't sent thank you messages to friends and relatives for the gifts they'd sent, and the last thing on my mind was finding the time to announce my daughter's arrival on my blog.

As any new parent will tell you, nothing turns your world upside-down like the arrival of a mini-human-being.

And *nothing* makes you realise how ludicrous the notion of 'having it all' is, than when it's 3 p.m. on a Tuesday afternoon and you're still in your pyjamas, holding your baby, surrounded by mess, and starving hungry...because you haven't had a minute to get dressed, stick the pots in the dishwasher, or grab a bite to eat.

'But we all have the same number of hours in a day as Beyonce!' I hear you cry.

Ah, yes. This slogan has been doing the viral rounds for a few years now. Yet another guilt-inducing statement that holds Beyonce aloft as some modern-day superwoman by which the rest of us females should be judged.

Okay, it is factually correct that we have the same amount of hours in a day as the beautiful Beyonce, but what most of us don't have is her staff and her money.

Only a small handful of us employ a nanny, a cook, a personal trainer, a stylist, a make-up artist, a chauffeur, and a personal assistant—or have millions of pounds in the bank at our disposal.

I love Beyonce. She's a powerhouse and an inspiration, <u>but</u> even she's not Superwoman. She just has a good team around her and plenty of money.

§

I can't remember exactly when I chose to be a little kinder to myself. But I do remember thinking that it wasn't going to be easy. And I was right, it hasn't been. It has, however, become much easier as time has marched on, and as I've made more effort to uncover where my feelings of guilt stem from.

Truth be told, I still experience guilt about something, almost every day. Mostly, it comes in waves, and it doesn't require much determination to mentally see it off. Other days, however, are much trickier and the guilt can feel overwhelming.

When a guilt attack happens, this is what I try and do: I pay attention to **how I'm speaking to myself** and make a conscious effort to stop the internal criticism.

I've found that a good question to ask myself when I spiral towards guilt, is this: 'Would I speak like this to a friend who feels bad about something?'

If the answer is no, I force myself to change my inner dialogue, and do my best to forgive myself and let the guilt go.

Secondly, I examine it. When I'm feeling bad about a situation, or guilty about something I have or haven't done, I try to figure out where the feelings of guilt have come from.

'Have I created it, is it justified, or is someone purposefully making me feel this way?'

When it comes to guilt, I've realised over the past few years that we are the main architects of it. No one is a harsher critic of me, than me! And I truly believe that this is probably the case for most, if not all, of us. Other people can make us feel guilty for things, but the choice to accept, amplify, or refuse the guilt comes down to us.

We choose what to let in and what standards to hold ourselves by.

As my dad once said to me many years ago: 'If at the end of the day you can look yourself in the eyes, in the mirror, you're doing alright.'

So, when those feelings hit you, forget 'throwing shade' at yourself. Instead, throw some light on the guilt.

Turn it over, examine it carefully, and ask, 'Where have you come from?'

§

Women are often their own worst enemies. I hate to say that, but I think most of us would agree that this is true to some degree.

Never is this more apparent than how we judge ourselves, and when deciding what we should take on.

We willingly heap pressure on our shoulders. We happily agree to more commitments. 'Yes' spills from our mouths before we've even given ourselves a moment to think. We hold ourselves to impossible standards. We berate ourselves for making any mistake. And the word 'no' is often one that sticks in our throats and refuses to come out.

Could it be that most of our guilt is of our own making? Does our guilt come down to wanting to be liked? Or being seen as 'nice' or 'pretty'? Could it really be that simple?

We've continually allowed society to make us feel guilty until we've accepted it as the norm. For thousands of years, the world has been told that it was all Eve's fault. If only she hadn't eaten that big, juicy apple! If she'd just done what she was supposed to, we'd have continued to live in blissful harmony.

Today, women still pay for Eve's alleged sins. Across the world, we're made to feel that *we* are the guilty party, when we're actually the victims.

It must stop.

We do not owe the world our niceness or prettiness. Our time on this planet is not supposed to be spent pursuing the ridiculous notion of perfection. We do not have to carry the world's problems on our shoulders anymore, nor accept the blame for most of them.

Isn't it time we made a concerted effort to liberate ourselves from guilt? Shouldn't we cut ourselves—*and* each other—some slack?

Just think how freeing and revolutionary that would be. I can even imagine Eve cheering us on.

'Pick Ups' to Take Away

♥ Female guilt has become our Achilles' heel. The more demanding modern life becomes, the harder we are on ourselves.

♥ We've been wrongly led to believe that our place in society is based on how nice we are to people and/or how nice we look. **It's not true.**

♥ Many of us are feeling guilty for **things we shouldn't feel guilty about** and we're carrying that burden around with us every single day.

♥ **We've been sold a lie**. We can't 'have it all' (or, at least, not all at once). Far from being empowering, this statement places immense pressure on us, causing frustration, exhaustion and masses of guilt. The sooner we realise this, the sooner our feelings of guilt will lessen.

♥ When we mistakenly believe we're letting ourselves down, or that we're not trying hard enough because we don't have it all, guilt flourishes.

♥ You may well have the same hours each day as Beyonce. Unlike her, however, you do not have a team of staff or seemingly-endless funds. Even Beyonce is not Superwoman (as fantastic as she is).

♥ We're not used to being kind to ourselves. It gets easier the more you put it into practice.

♥ When feelings of guilt arise, two things can help. 1) **Change how you speak to yourself** (if you're not speaking as kindly as you would to a friend, it's time to change your inner dialogue); 2) **Examine it!** Where has the guilt come from? Is it justified, or is someone else making you feel this way?

♥ **We are often the manufacturers of our guilt.** Other people may try to make us feel guilty, but it's up to us whether we accept or reject their efforts.

♥ **We're our own harshest critics.** Few of us would hold anyone else to the impossible standards that we apply to ourselves.

♥ Guilt has become engrained in our female psyche. For thousands of years, women have been held accountable for many of the world's sins and made to feel bad about themselves in the process. It's time we were kinder and more forgiving to ourselves and each other.

♥ We're not here to create perfect lives. We do not owe the world our niceness or prettiness. We do not have to shoulder blame and guilt anymore.

♥ Guilt has become the things that shackles us. *It's time we cut ourselves free.*

DREAD

Dread

'Ageing is out of your control. How you handle it,
though, is in your hands.'

~ Diane Von Furstenberg

We all have things that we dread.

Going to the dentist, checking our bank statements after Christmas or, if you're anything like me, having to talk to another human being you don't know very well over the phone (give me emails or text messages any day!).

Dread.

It overwhelms us when we have to do/face up to things that we don't want to. Things that don't make us feel good, but which need to be dealt with.

Dread is also a perfect breeding ground for other unpleasant emotions we'd rather not feel, with anxiety and fear being two of its stable-mates; because, when dread comes to play, it never comes alone.

I think dread has an unfair reputation. Whilst it may make us feel uncomfortable and anxious, it's **also a brilliant reminder that we need to tackle something.**

A bit like fear, it's impossible to hide from dread because it's persistent. It never gives up. Dread is a lingerer—there to make sure you've tackled the very thing that's created it in the first place.

And if you don't?

Well, it grows. It grows from a quiet 'you know it's there in the pit of your stomach' feeling into the 'can't sleep, can't stop thinking about it' horror. It ruins your sleep as well as your peace of mind. That's when you can no longer ignore it.

Like an alarm clock, dread will shriek louder and louder until you get up and face whatever it is you have to do. And just like the other unpleasant emotions we feel, dread does not like to be ignored. If you keep shutting the door in its face, you could be in for a rude awakening when it turns into a nuisance.

The good news is: dread quickly disappears as soon we take action. All we need to do is tackle whatever it is that's causing our worry or stress and it will leave us alone (and we always know what that thing is). I admit, this isn't as easy as it sounds.

A bit of a rebel at heart, I'm not very good at doing things I don't want to do. Even when I know they have to be done. I'm someone who likes to do things at my own pace and in my own time. Reluctantly, I've become much better at it.

As an indicator that tells you what you need to tackle in your life, you won't find a better one than dread.

Want inner peace? Then tackle the things you're putting off.

As a freelancer, there are many things that crop up in my work life that make me feel uncomfortable. Things that I need to do but which I really, *really* don't want to do.

From chasing up late/unpaid invoices to keeping on top of my finances; from asking for more money to resolving problems with challenging clients; there are so many things that make me squirm with anxiety and which take me out of my comfort zone.

Sadly, the world of self-employment, as fantastic as it is, isn't all leisurely meetings over coffee or taking time off when you fancy it.

It's bloody tough.

I read not so long ago that the most successful people have one simple thing in common: when it comes to tackling their to–do list, they **always deal with the difficult things first.** *They get them out of the way.*

A few years ago, I thought I'd try this myself. Instead of cracking on with the nice bits of my job, or the less-pressing issues that I didn't mind sorting, I forced myself—and I sincerely mean that—to start my working day dealing with all the stuff I was dreading *first.*

Much to my amazement, it worked. It cleared my mind *so* quickly and I still swear by this method of working today.

Getting the hard, the messy, the painful, the difficult, or the uncomfortable stuff out of the way as quickly as possible **makes life easier.** It kills the feelings of dread before they have an opportunity to shriek; it removes worry and helps lessen fears.

Dealing with dread is like taking foul-tasting medicine. You might hate the thought of doing it, but you know that it's for your own good and that, in the end, it will make you feel better.

Next time you wake up dreading the day and all that awaits you, give it a try. Make a list of the things that are causing you turmoil and make it your mission to get those sorted before you think about anything else.

I promise it will help.

'But what if it's as bad as I think?' you may ask. 'What if doing or facing the thing I dread is as awful, terrifying or embarrassing as my imagination makes it out to be?'

Let's unpack this…

We've already established that, generally, **the things**

we dread are things we have to do, whether we like it or not.

So, isn't it better just to get on with them and accept the reality? Isn't it better to face whatever it is that's causing us pain, particularly when we know that it isn't going to disappear until we do?

Allowing dread to fester puts our imaginations into overdrive. The more we put something off, the worse it begins to look. The more we try to hide away from something, the more it haunts us. Our imaginations take our feelings of dread and all the worry and fear that goes along with them and they go to town, creating nightmarish images in our mind that reflect back to us what we think and believe to be true.

If we think of something in a dark light, our imagination will dish up images that serve these thoughts, presenting everything we dread to us as unappealing at best, and terrifying at worst.

The more **we allow our feelings of dread to fester, the worst these images become**.

For instance, consider completely-normal, run-of-the-mill smear tests. I don't think any woman would say that she looks forward to having one. But once you're there and the nurse is jabbering away to you about her recent holiday, and you're both laughing in solidarity about how awkward a smear test is, you soon realise that there's no need to dread them at all.

Yet there are women today—intelligent, rational, brilliant women—who have *never* been for a smear test in their lives, simply because the picture they've created in their own minds is too dreadful for them to bear.

These women are risking their health (please, please, don't ever let this be you) because of the images they've created that they believe to be true.

And yet this simple test could save their lives. A bit of discomfort, a bit of embarrassment, a bit of pain. Like it or not, we must occasionally experience these things from time to time for our greater good.

It's worth remembering that most things in life are never as bad as we *imagine* them to be.

§

Uncomfortable situations or conversations aside, what is it that us women seem to dread the most?

One word: *ageing*.

We need to change our approach to ageing and stop seeing it as something to fear. We need to instead **see it as something to celebrate.**

I know, for many of us, this can be hard. We live in a world that values youth and beauty, seemingly above other things. A world that thinks it's perfectly acceptable to use teenage girls to advertise and sell products aimed at older women. Retailers' shelves are packed with 'anti-ageing' products that promise us the elixir of youth.

The message is clear: *women must do their very best to hold back the years as best as they can.*

It's not surprising that we dread getting older. It's a reasonable worry in many respects for women, because the older we get, the more invisible we seem to become.

It's not right that women have money to spend but can't always spend it, because the high street seems to cater for a younger female market, even though our spending power is potentially much greater.

It's ridiculous that talented actresses appear to vanish from our TV screens because they've reached the 'age ceiling'. Or that brilliant female TV presenters are replaced by much younger women—or even older men—when they get to a certain age.

This is what often happens. This is what we see and hear. As a woman, getting older is seen as one of the worst things that can happen to us.

Hide the years! Cover the signs! Try not to age!

Is it any wonder women dread the question, 'How old are you?'

I hear you sigh. I'm sighing, too. It's uncomfortable reading because it's bloody unfair.

And *ridiculous*. Really, really ridiculous.

The way I see it, we have two choices. We can carry on as we are, dreading our advancing years and allowing society to steal happiness from our lives, or we can decide that we're not going to play that game and do our best to challenge the status quo.

I know which option I prefer.

If we want to age well and live our lives with freedom and happiness, we must change our mindset. We must stop looking at ageing as something that steals beauty and opportunities from us and **ensure the opposite becomes the reality**.

It's that simple.

In a matter of months, I'll turn forty. It's something I'm very excited about, and something I refuse to dread. Some younger women may not see this as a cause for celebration, but I could not disagree more.

I'm planning the *works*. There will be a party and I'm planning to wear a fabulously fancy frock. There'll be cake and balloons. I may even give a speech.

I will see my forties in, not with tears of sadness, but tears of joy. The same way I hope to bring in every new decade, if I'm lucky enough to see them.

Think of the way young children celebrate their birthdays. They're excited, giddy, and they count down the days until they're a year older. This joyful attitude towards getting older can be ours, too. We should *never* be embarrassed or depressed about how old we are or will be on our next birthday. Stuff what society might try and tell us. To deny our age is like slapping our maker in the face, for allowing us to exist on this planet a little longer.

Claim your age. Celebrate it. Shout it from the goddamn rooftops if you can and make an effort to appreciate where you are in your life right now. None of us know how long we have on this earth.

§

We do not lose our value as we age. Read that repeatedly if you need to.

Regardless of what we've been led to believe, our value does not go down with our advancing years. It actually goes up.

Wrinkles. Grey hair. We shouldn't dread them. Like everything else associated with getting older, **we just need to change how we see them.**

Fight the external signs of advancing years or embrace them. It's completely up to you.

Getting older does not mean that people will no longer find you attractive or lose interest in what you have to say. It doesn't mean fewer opportunities or less fun.

The person who determines this, however, is you. It shouldn't be determined on how many times you've travelled around the sun.

Relax, enjoy life, and let the years tick by. Stop worrying about your age; stop dreading the turn of each decade. Take each number with a pinch of salt and choose to see every birthday as the perfect excuse to have a party, or to bring your favourite people together.

You cannot stop ageing. None of us can. And who really wants to? Look at the alternative!

Women have been made to feel bad about getting older for too long. We've been made to *dread* living longer.

When you stop to think about that, isn't that awful?

Truly awful, when there are people fighting for their lives and babies breathing their last breaths.

Companies <u>want</u> you to dread your next birthday, because then they can sell you things and make money out of you. There are industries out there that would go bust if we regarded old age as a blessing, not a curse, because they've made a fortune out of our insecurities and feelings of worthlessness.

Don't let them.

If you want to freeze your wrinkles into submission with a vat of Botox, go for it. If you want to rub expensive anti-wrinkle creams into your face every day, knock yourself out. Your life, your call.

But, please, don't be conned into thinking you can stop the ageing process. Or believe that looking younger or smoother will make you more valuable as a human being—or even that it will make you happier.

Here's a radical idea: **just aim to be the very best version of you at any age.** At every age. Whatever that looks like to you.

This is what I'm striving for. I don't want to look 18 when I'm 40, or 25 when I hit 50. I don't want to go back in time and do my twenties, or even my thirties, all over again. All I want is to feel my best, whatever my age.

Here are some things to help you feel happier and more inspired when it comes to getting older...

1) **Find some role models**. Look beyond the stereotypes we're frequently given when it comes to women and <u>find your own role models</u>. You won't have to search the internet for long to come across incredible women of all ages doing the most amazing things. And don't forget about the brilliant women in your own life either, the ones you love, know, or speak to on a regular basis.

Find women that ignore the rules. Find women that defy convention. Let them inspire you to be your best and most authentic self. The world is full of women enjoying their age and living their best lives.

These women continue to inspire me: Oprah Winfrey, Monica Bellucci, Michelle Obama, Nora Ephron, Madonna, Carmen Dell'Orefice, Tracee Ellis Ross, Sharon Stone, Vivienne Westwood, Michelle Pfeiffer, Tao Porchon–Lynch, Jennifer Lopez, JK Rowling, Meryl Streep and Cheryl Strayed.

2) **Make friends with women of all ages**. My dear friend, Pat, is in her super-seventies and I have learned more from my conversations with her than I have with anyone my own age. Age really is no barrier when it comes to connecting and friendships.

Mix up your friendship groups, introduce yourself to new people, and make an effort to befriend, support and learn from women of all ages.

3) **See each decade as a new opportunity.** Each decade of our lives comes with different challenges. My thirties have been consumed by pregnancy, being a mum to young children, and navigating the world of self-employment. What will my forties hold…?

Who knows? But I'm looking forward to finding out.

4) **Ignore everything you're told about age.** Don't allow the world to make you feel insecure. Make your own rules.

Set your own standards. Ignore convention. You can, and will, be fabulous at any age, if you believe this to be true.
5) **Believe that life, and YOU, will continue to get better and better.** Eleanor Roosevelt said: 'Beautiful, young people are accidents of nature. But beautiful, old people are works of art.'

I couldn't have put it better myself. Ageing is *not* a dirty word, nor something to fight or dread. Far from it, in fact. It's a gift.

No wrinkles, or a face full of wrinkles. Whichever, we're all here to make as many memories as we can. The longer, the better, I say. Wouldn't you agree?

On my fortieth birthday, there'll be no hiding away. No 'pretending it's not happening' or knocking a year off my age. I'll kiss goodbye to my thirties—which have been more incredible than I could ever have imagined—and welcome my forties with open arms.

No dread, just excitement...lots of excitement.

The next time someone tells me they're about to enter a new decade, I'll make sure to tell them how fabulous that is and how fabulous *they* are.

I want to live as long as I can. I want to squeeze in as much as I can, whether I'm 40, 50, 60, 70...

Just think of all the memories awaiting us! How on earth can any of us dread that?

'Pick Ups' To Take Away

♥ Dread appears when we feel we must do or face something we don't want to.

♥ It can make us feel awful, uncomfortable, anxious and even fearful, but it's a brilliant reminder that we need to tackle something—and soon.

♥ Dread disappears quickly when we take action. Tackle whatever it is that's causing you worry and stress and dread will leave you alone.

♥ For a happier, less stressful life, tackle the things you dread *first*.

♥ Getting the hard stuff out of the way as quickly as possible **makes life easier**.

♥ Allowing feelings of dread to fester sends our imaginations into overdrive. The more we put something off, the worse it begins to look. The more we try to hide away from something, the more it haunts us.

♥ If you're a woman who dreads the thought of a smear test, please, don't risk your life. There's nothing to it and it only takes a few minutes. Make an appointment right now if it's due.

♥ A bit of discomfort, a bit of embarrassment, a bit of pain…we must occasionally experience these things in life for our own good.

♥ Remember, most things in life are *never* as bad as we imagine or dread them to be.

♥ Many women dread ageing, but how we approach getting older is down to us.

♥ You have two choices: dread your advancing years or enjoy them. Only one option will make you happy.

♥ When it comes to ageing, we must change our mindset and stop seeing it as something that steals things from us.

♥ Claim your age, celebrate it, and be grateful that you're still alive.

♥ **We do not lose our value as we age.**

♥ Choose to be the best *you* at any age.

♥ Think of all the memories yet to be made! How can any of us dread that?

POWERLESSNESS

Powerlessness

*'Wherever you are is your circle of influence, your platform.
This is where your power lies. Every day you are
showing people who you are. You are letting your
life speak for you.'*

~ Oprah Winfrey

As I delivered my son, Leo, into the world on a cold, grey,
January day, I had an epiphany.

A moment of revelation so inspiring, it changed how I
thought about myself—and other women—forever.

I dug deep during his birth and, for the first time ever,
I truly recognised the magnitude of my own power. In
a hi-tech delivery suite, on a hospital bed, crouched on
all fours, I felt the immense pain of established labour.
I worked through the by-now almost unbearable final
contractions, knowing that at any moment my son would
be with me.

For a split-second, I left the mental birthing bubble I'd
inhabited for twelve hours and had a profound thought:
'I've crossed a pain barrier, the likes of which I've never
known…but it's not breaking me. Wow! I truly am
powerful.'

That 'aha!' moment was not just a turning point in my
labour (which, thankfully, saw Leo arrive safely just a few
minutes later), but a turning point in my life.

Even though I'd been totally consumed by the birthing
process, in that moment, I recognised the undeniable
truth: I knew that Leo's birth had changed me forever—

and not just because I was now a mum to *two* incredible mini-humans.

If I'd had even the *slightest* doubt about the power women possess, it was well and truly obliterated.

We're not meant to think this, of course. The world isn't generally a fan of women who claim their power. In most cases, society would rather have us believe that, far from being powerful, we're actually power*less*.

Yet, within you and I, within our daughters and granddaughters, lies a deep well of power. **We are all so much more powerful than we know.**

§

The world would like us to believe that powerful women are threatening. During the last few decades we've seen progress with regards to women's safety and equality. Despite this, you only have to flick through the pages of a magazine or switch on the TV for a few minutes to find depressing examples of how fragile and vulnerable our power still is.

Sadly, there's no getting away from it. We face immense challenges because of our gender.

I can remember gazing at Elsie, when she was just an hour old, as she lay peacefully sleeping in the tiny hospital crib. As I stood over her, feeling immense pride and awe, watching her little chest rise and fall with each breath, I suddenly found myself silently apologising to her for the many things she'd have to encounter throughout her life, just because she was born a girl.

'I'm so sorry, darling,' I whispered. 'I'm so, so sorry.'

As a mother, I hate that my daughter isn't as safe in this world as my son, just because she happens to be female. I hate that her power may be regarded as something to be minimised whilst my son's will be seen as something to be encouraged.

I could scream at the absolute unfairness of it all, but what good would that do?

It isn't right that powerful men get to make decisions about our incredible bodies, or that we are still not safe to walk down a street at night.

It's outrageous that many employers think it's acceptable to pay us less than our male colleagues, or that working mums are struggling to make ends meet because they have to part with most of their wages just to cover childcare costs.

And it breaks my heart when I read about rape victims having their underwear examined in court, or when a famous man found guilty of rape or domestic violence is welcomed back into society with open arms, his crimes conveniently forgotten.

Our power is forever under attack, being minimised or it's snatched away from us. Is it any wonder so many of us wrongly believe that we don't have any real power at all?

Ask any woman about a time in her life in which she felt powerless and you will get, in most cases, not just one story, but several. Every woman I know has stories to tell about such things, including me.

There have been many times in my life when I've felt powerless: in threatening circumstances, manipulative relationships or work situations.

Walking down the street. Standing at a bar. Sitting on a train. We face danger so often it's become second nature to walk more quickly when daylight begins to fade, or to check our female friends got home as safely as we did after a night out.

We're so used to being treated unfairly that we often don't bother to ask for a pay rise or expect things to be different.

But things can be different.

They *must* be different.

I knew when I had Elsie that it was my duty to do more to try to make the world a fairer, safer place for her. To do my best to equip her with the knowledge and skills she will need to navigate her way through this unbalanced world with confidence and strong self-belief.

It's a huge undertaking. But, it's an essential part of parenting, and a task I take *very* seriously. For our daughters need, and deserve, to know that they *are* powerful, regardless of the nonsense society or the world tries to tell them.

And so do we.

§

If we're faced with injustice and unfairness everywhere we turn, it's not surprising that so many of us become blind to the power that **already lies within us**.

It's not surprising that so many of choose to reject, ignore or stifle our power and forget about the many ways in which we can make a huge difference—not just to our own lives, but also to the lives of others.

Perhaps you wrongly believe, like I once did, that you don't have what it takes to step up and claim your rightful place in the world. Or maybe you're so exhausted from all the constant challenges you face as a woman, you've given up trying to shape or influence anything. *You're done with it all. You've had enough.*

It may be that, at some point, you suffered something so horrific or unfair, that you feel like you've lost all your power. And you've no inclination to try and get it back or any idea how you'd even begin.

Many of us are tired and frazzled, as well as angry, confused and frightened. We're frustrated by the same old outcomes. Exhausted from continually pounding on closed doors and trying to smash our way through the toughest of glass ceilings. Being a woman, unfortunately, means that we often have to battle in ways men do not. We have to think about keeping ourselves safe in ways men could never imagine.

We cannot, and must not, give up.

I know it's hard—*so* incredibly hard—but our work has only just begun.

Let's claim our power back.

Even if we don't believe we're powerless, we may think that any power we do have is limited. This is simply not true. Whilst we undoubtedly face challenges we should never have to face, we must also **take responsibility** for the power we willingly hand over to others. All this does is leave ourselves open to attack.

On occasion, **we minimise our own power**. As you read through the following list, be honest with yourself and acknowledge the thoughts you may have had or scenarios you may have found yourself in.

It may feel unpleasant but please stick with it, because the purpose of this is to hopefully show you that **there is** *so* **much potential for positive change...**

* Staying quiet when you know you should speak up.
* Putting up with someone else's inappropriate behaviour.
* Staying in unhealthy, abusive or toxic relationships.
* Talking negatively to yourself.
* Believing you're powerless and acting accordingly.

* Gossiping about other women instead of defending them.
* Giving away too much of yourself for too little, or even for free.
* Wrongly believing that women are only powerful when playing by society's rules.
* Not looking after your finances.
* Not taking responsibility for the choices you make.
* Believing it's better or safer to fit in rather than daring to stand out.
* Comparing yourself unfairly with other women, instead of appreciating who you are and what you have to offer.
* Falsely believing that life is something that happens *to* you.
* Hoping for the best and keeping your fingers crossed that things will change for the better, on their own.
* Feeling too embarrassed or ashamed to ask for help.
* Not believing that you're good enough.
* Believing that what you do doesn't matter.
* Allowing the men in your life to make all the decisions.
* Not allowing yourself to dream or to believe that you *can* create the life you want.
* Staying put in jobs, relationships and situations, even though you know they're no good for you.
* Being too scared to be your authentic self, in case you're rejected.
* Spending too much money on material things you don't really need.
* Feeling bad if you say no and always feeling obliged to say yes.
* Allowing motherhood to consume you.

* Staying in your comfort zone instead of trying new things.
* Allowing anyone to be your friend instead of choosing the people you invite into your life wisely.
* Allowing yourself to feel overwhelmed.
* Turning on others.

That's a long list, isn't it? I could have continued! Hopefully, it gives you an indication of the many ways in which we can throw away our power and limit our happiness and success, without even realising it.

Consciously or not, many of us invite others to treat us badly; we accept things we should never allow and diminish our power in a variety of ways.

The good news is, once we begin to recognise these things, it's much easier than we may imagine to turn things around.

It's difficult for me to share what I'm about to. However, owning up to the person I used to be and taking responsibility for my own unhealthy behaviour is important. Not just for my own development, but to demonstrate how quickly our lives can, and do, change for the better when we dare to claim our power.

We can't expect life to shower us with good fortune when we treat ourselves in ways that are detrimental to our happiness and success. It's just not the way life works.

I used to be a self-pitying victim. Pathetically so, in fact. Many years ago, in my late teens, I was *that* young woman—who believed life was terribly unkind to her. Who forever felt hard done by. I smiled outwardly and said all the right things, but inside I was furious at the world and the hand I'd been given.

I was *that* person (we all know at least one) who would continually wail in despair, 'Why do these things always happen to me?!', as if nothing bad or challenging had ever happened to anyone else. I was miserable, damaged and hurt; to be fair, at the time, I didn't know any better.

I was a young woman, trying desperately to make sense of things. Astonishingly, the more I believed bad things only ever happened to me, the more life appeared to show me how right I was. It became a self-fulfilling prophecy.

'Life's always out to get me!' I'd say to myself.

I really believed it.

But the truth, however hard it is now to admit, is that most, if not all, of my misfortune **was actually created by me!**

I was the one making the appalling choices and placing myself continuously in harm's way.

I perceived the world as a dark place, and so naturally sought out people who believed the same.

My life was not a mess because I'd been dealt a bad hand by the universe. **It was a mess because I'd allowed it to be that way. I'd created it.**

I was a lost soul back then. A young woman with so much potential and with so much to be thankful for, but who could not see it. I was blind to my own power.

Never feeling good enough, I did what most people naturally do when they feel that way. I began to self-destruct. Nothing and no one could stop me.

It wasn't long before I succeeded.

By the time I was twenty, I'd almost thrown away any chance of ever being happy. Of having a successful future, glittering career, or the company of loving, decent people in my life.

With a bit of help from people on their own self-destructive missions, I did a great job of almost ruining my future.

My late teens were a horrible time.

I did things I'm not proud of and spent time with people that were definitely no good for me. It's a period of my life I'm more than happy to forget, and yet, in so many ways, I believe it was the making of me.

Twenty years on and I've learned to see that what happened was actually a blessing. All my dreadful, foolish mistakes have helped to shape me into a better person (at least I like to think so). Destroying my life was disastrous at the time, but it also gave me the perfect opportunity to rebuild. Please don't ever be in any doubt about this—we *all* have the power to create a much happier future.

True, we can't go back in time to change things, but we can continually evaluate, learn and grow from them. This is what life is all about.

Back then, on the cusp of womanhood, I wrongly thought I was powerless. That life is something that just *happens*, and that blessings are bestowed on you *or not*.

But it was actually my power, my actions, my decisions, my thinking and my beliefs, that blew my life up and shattered it to smithereens.

Oh, the irony! I learned that it takes just as much power to destroy your life as it does to make it flourish. It's a lesson I've never forgotten and one I hope you'll take note of, too.

Only one person creates your life. And that, in case you haven't figured it out by now, **is you**! You are the author of your story. The only person who can decide to make or break you.

We cannot control what happens to us, and sometimes what happens to us can be awful or terrifying, soul destroying or unjust.

Even then, when life is at its worst, we *always* have power in the choices we make and the thoughts we have. Our thinking forms our decisions, which form the habits that shape our lives.

Every day we make all manner of decisions. Where we might live, to how to respond to someone's email. We can choose to go down a path that's covered in potholes or pick the one that's smoother and prettier but perhaps not as well-trodden.

Your happiness and success are largely up to you.

When I began to rebuild my life at the age of twenty, I made a conscious effort to change my mindset. Since then I've worked hard—*really* hard—to be a better human being. To become a version of Katie that I can be proud of, and which my loved ones can be proud of, too.

Within months of trying my best to turn things around, good things—*really* good things—started to happen. I met an incredible man (my wonderful husband), and I began to envisage a future for myself that looked exciting and full of opportunity. I learned to be braver, more determined and kinder, and less materialistic.

From the gutter, literally at rock bottom, I began to slowly rise. Life became lighter and brighter and I've never looked back.

All that said, I am still a work in progress. I make mistakes (some of which are absolute corkers), and I regularly encounter challenges that knock me for six.

Life can often feel impossible, or it presents us with curved balls that we struggle to handle.

The difference now is that I no longer believe I am powerless to change things. I *know* that my life is of my own making, and I'm determined to make it as fantastic and fulfilling as I can.

§

So, how do we fight our feelings of powerlessness? How can we create lives we are proud of? These are just some of the many ways I've managed to do just that.

1) Have courage

The more I challenge myself, personally or professionally, the more powerful I feel and the happier I become. They say that *'fortune favours the brave';* from experience, I believe this to be true.

My husband, Jamie, surprised me once when he said, in his opinion, my courage was my greatest personal attribute. His comment remains one of the loveliest things anyone has ever said about me.

If you only take away one piece of advice from this chapter, let it be this: **courage is your ticket to living an exciting and fulfilling life.**

Put yourself out there. Be prepared to fall occasionally. And face whatever frightens you.

I promise that you won't ever regret it.

2) Use your voice (wisely)

Our voices are amongst our greatest tools, yet many of us remain silent about too many important things.

Speak up and speak the truth. Share your story, own your feelings, ask for whatever it is you need—and, please, never be afraid to speak up for someone else or for an important cause.

We owe it to ourselves, to the next generation of women, and to our ancestors, to be as vocal and as honest as we can.

3) Own your space

Many women metaphorically (some, physically) shrink, because they're worried they may offend or upset people. They play it small because they fear being rejected or ridiculed.

Please, don't do this.

At my husband's fortieth birthday party, a friend of mine, when she saw what I was wearing—a green mini-dress covered in sequins—cheekily asked if it was my party or my husband's. With a friendly wink, I said, 'Well, you either go big or you go home!'

I think this is a fabulous motto to live by. Every woman deserves to own her space, to stand out and be seen.

Some people, however, may not like it when you do. They may feel threatened or envious. They might mock you or try their very best to 'pop your bubble'.

Just ignore them and carry on. The world *needs* you to be your best, authentic self. Anything else is just a waste.

4) Be your best self

With confidence comes power, and the easiest way to demonstrate confidence and high self-esteem is **by making an effort to always present your best self.**

People treat us as we treat ourselves. So, treat yourself properly, and **give yourself the attention you deserve.**

Make an effort with your appearance (not for anyone else—for you!); be mindful of your body language; use your voice wisely and make sure your style demonstrates who you truly are.

And if you struggle with this kind of thing? Go and get some help.

I recently worked with a stylist and have now learned which colours suit me best and which 'style personality' accurately reflects me (I'm a 'romantic natural' in case you're interested). This proved an absolute *revelation* for me.

If you feel that your personal presentation is lacking

in some area(s), find someone that can help you make changes. Honestly, you'll feel fabulous as a result.

5) Educate yourself

My gran, Peggy, was a big fan of education, and for a very good reason. **She agreed that knowledge *is* power.**

One of the best things any of us can do to help ourselves, is to **never stop learning.** Today, in this digital age, where information is at our fingertips in a fraction of a second, there really is no excuse to not boost your grey matter.

As you'd probably expect, I'm a big fan of the written word; I'm always reading books or blog posts. But my husband swears by YouTube for guidance and knowledge when he's struggling with anything from DIY to cooking. Other people I know listen to podcasts or they watch presentations delivered by some of the world's greatest minds.

It's never been easier to continue to learn. Keep at it and watch your personal power grow.

6) Change how you talk to yourself

I've spoken about this already. I really can't emphasise it enough.

Changing a negative, critical voice into a more positive and loving one, <u>will change your life.</u>

This is the single best thing I've ever done for myself. It's worked wonders for me.

What do you think about yourself? How do you treat *you*? How do you allow others to treat you? How do you perceive the world—positively, or negatively? If it's the latter, you need to change this, because everything stems from here.

Want to feel more powerful, valued and loved? Then make a start by telling yourself that you <u>are</u> powerful, valued and loved. Because, whether they're right or wrong, we always believe the messages we tell ourselves to be the absolute truth.

7) Live by your own standards

To me, being truly powerful is creating a life that works for us. A life that fulfils our individual needs, challenges us, and which brings us immense joy.

So, **make your own rules**. Decide what's important to you (and your family, if applicable) and live your life by this framework.

You don't have to live your life like everyone else or stay in the town you grew up in. You don't have to keep up with your peers or spend your days working in a job you hate because it made your parents happy.

As an adult, one of the most beautiful things we grow into **is our freedom**. Use it wisely and, if nothing else, **make sure *your* life works for *you*.** (The same goes for parenting.)

8) Don't let fear get the better of you

I hate to imagine how many dreams have never come to fruition because of fear. Or how many lives have not been enjoyed to their fullest, because of this particularly strong mental beast.

There's no doubt fear can render us absolutely powerless, but to have any chance of overpowering this emotion, it's important to not think about it in that way. As I said earlier, **fear can be a brilliant motivator if we choose to see it as such**.

For me, fear has become an ally. Whenever it rears its head, I take it as a green light. I choose to see fear as a sign that I need to be brave and that a leap of faith awaits.

9) When you're overwhelmed, do *something*

At least once a month there's a day when I feel like

I'm sinking under all the stuff I have to do.

I become overwhelmed by life and my many responsibilities to a point that I almost can't think straight. On days like these, I used to cry or hide in bed, but that didn't make things any better.

I now choose to live by this golden rule instead: whenever you feel overwhelmed, **take action and do something**. It doesn't have to be a big action—it doesn't even have to be 'work' of any sort; but just **go and do something.**

It's easy to feel stuck and powerless when life gets the better of you; whenever overwhelm strikes, get your stagnant energy moving by acting. For example, if your house is a tip and you feel like it would be easier to climb a mountain than get on top of the cleaning, just concentrate on tidying one small area. If your inbox is full, give yourself half-an-hour to reply to as many of those emails as you can. If you're exhausted because you've been up all night with a baby and you're too tired to cook, order a takeaway.

When overwhelm strikes, just concentrate on doing something. It's the best way I know to get out of the fog… which leads me nicely onto the next tip:

10) Ask for help

I think that one of the biggest myths women believe is that asking for help will make them appear powerless.

But it doesn't. Far from it.

Powerful women recognise when they need help and aren't afraid to ask for it. They're happy to admit when they're struggling and choose to seek out solutions to their problems as soon as they can—instead of believing that they should be able to 'do it all'.

Powerful women aren't embarrassed to admit that

they may need help. **They feel that taking control, rather than remaining stuck, empowers them** – even if it means bringing someone else to the situation.

Learn from these women. Whenever you're in a pickle, take a deep breath and ask for help.

11) Put yourself first

Women are notoriously good at looking after others but rubbish at looking after themselves.

We need to try harder with our self-care. It's impossible to feel powerful when we don't feel we have anything left to give. Start putting yourself first.

At first, it may feel weird and you may feel incredibly guilty. But remember, it's no one else's job to make you feel better. That responsibility is yours alone.

Be protective of your energy, talents and time, and be wary of allowing anyone into your life that seeks to drain them.

As Iyanla Vanzant so brilliantly said: 'You have to fill your cup first before it can overflow for others.'

I couldn't put it better myself.

§

Finally, it's time to talk about the elephant in the room. The thing that none of us really wants to admit to, but deep down, know and understand only too well. We are not as supportive or kind enough to one another as we should be. Nor as we need to be, in order that we all thrive.

A few years ago, the world-renowned Australian writer and intellectual Germaine Greer was speaking in my hometown of Barnsley. One of the things she talked about during that evening has stayed with me ever since.

As a marginalised group within society, we have turned on each other instead of turning on the system

that oppresses us.

And what's more, we're continually encouraged to do this, by the very people who enforce our oppression.

Women have been told that, in order to survive, we must compete **against each other** for men and for work. We've been trained to see other women as sworn enemies that we need to defeat, rather than allies.

Thankfully, I know many women who do not think this way. However, *I also know many that do.*

Like most of us, I've been on the receiving end of some horrible female behaviour. At school, in the workplace, and even from supposed 'friends'.

The hatred of some women towards others is a *huge* problem, and one that we *all* need to be honest about and courageous enough to address, if we're to have any chance of improving things.

I don't want to see the worst in our sex, but neither can I pretend there's not a problem when there so clearly is. If we want to thrive, achieve true equality, and create a safer world for our daughters, we must stop seeing each other as the enemy and learn to like each other again.

When we're all in the same boat, it seems ludicrous to me that so many of us choose to rock it. We're bound to make mistakes at times...*it's inevitable.* Gossiping about another woman, for example, or criticising a famous female for how she looks when she appears on TV.

It's natural to feel threatened or jealous of other women from time to time. Centuries of being oppressed has done this to us.

We're more than capable of building a sisterhood we can be proud of. There are things we can all do to support each other and strengthen our collective power:

1) Offer a helping hand

When you see another woman struggling, do the right thing and step in. If she's battling with a fractious toddler, don't do as I did before I was a mother and roll your eyes as you smugly walk away, thinking it will never happen to you (I'm deeply ashamed of this; karma made sure I got my just desserts!).

Give the mother a warm smile and say something along the lines of, 'Toddlers! They know how to cause a commotion, don't they? My eldest was just the same. You're doing a great job, by the way.'

If you know another woman is feeling low, send her a message and check she's okay.

If another woman wants to do your job, be kind and share some of your knowledge. It will make her feel inspired and supported.

Help other women, wherever and whenever you can. It's the right—and kind—thing to do.

2) Stop engaging in unpleasant female behaviour

You know what I'm talking about. The gossip. The slander. The leaving other women out, the ghosting of a past friend, the looking other women up and down.

We can all be drawn into unpleasant conversations, but we need to stop such toxic habits that have been the female 'norm' for so long. This behaviour, which we've all been guilty of at some point in our lives, is truly horrid.

We deserve better than this.

Next time you find yourself condemning another woman behind her back, or catch yourself behaving unfairly against a member of our sex, stop and ask yourself: 'Is this *really* how I want to be?'

Let's face it, when we're horrible about/to another human being, it says much more about us than it does about them.

3) Talk to one another and be honest.

When it comes to female conversation, in an ideal world, we should be able to tell each other anything. We should be able to talk openly about the many issues we face, knowing that the other woman will understand and support us.

We *should* be able to.

Often, however, our conversations, if we're not careful, can turn into a battle of one-upmanship, or be full of nothing but the latest gossip, rather than creating genuine connection.

It's not always easy to open up to each other. We may believe that our secrets are not safe with another woman (sometimes, unfortunately, we may be right), or we feel too embarrassed to share them.

It could be that sharing makes us feel vulnerable, or we mistakenly believe that another woman will never understand our innermost thoughts—or worse, use them to judge us.

We're great at small talk and fantastic at gossip, but we're not always as good at being open with one another.

We need to talk—not *more*, just *better*.

The more frankly we can talk and the more we allow ourselves to be vulnerable—by revealing our truest, deepest parts to another woman—the more connected and powerful we'll all feel.

Today, we're constantly bombarded with images of what perfect lives and perfect bodies look like, thanks to social media. It's easy to think that we don't measure up, or to worry that we're not like everyone else, which is exactly why it's more important than ever to be as honest and transparent with each other as we can.

Finally, if you have a problem with another woman, consider talking to her about it. From time to time we're all guilty of hurting others unintentionally or being particularly sensitive to other people's actions. Wires can become crossed and people make mistakes; it's vital that we talk to one another to rectify misunderstandings and put things right as soon as we can, before situations escalate and feelings spiral out of control. Try and clear the air as politely and as kindly as you can.

4) Admire, respect and praise other women

They're the best things we can do for each other, after recognising our similarities and working out our differences.

We should always aim to admire and praise other women, not just because it's a great way to find brilliant, positive role models; more importantly, **it's the right thing to do.**

We live in a world that encourages catfights between females. It's common to open a magazine and see two women wearing the same outfit displayed alongside each other, with the caption 'Who wore it best?'.

'The sisterhood' is *not* an impossible dream. We're all capable of making it a reality.

One of the best things about being a freelance writer and blogger is meeting new people. I've been introduced to some truly fascinating, intelligent, passionate, talented women from all walks of life—many of which have become great friends of mine.

Freelancing has taught me how important it really is to admire, respect and praise other women.

We *need* support and encouragement from each other. We *need* to know that other women want us to succeed and be happy, to know without question that they've got our backs.

We've got so much already against us. Why make things harder?

Know that we're stronger together. It's true, we are. It's as simple as that.

5) Be the example you want to see.

Elsie is my mirror. She shows me my good things and highlights the bad. If ever I've questioned whether I have any influence as a human being, woman and mother, Elsie has shown me that this should never be in any doubt.

We have more power and influence than we realise; if we want to change people's lives for the better...indeed, if we want to change the world, **we must set better examples.**

Be the mother you never had.

Be the role model you want to see.

Your influence is unquestionable.

6) Give back and do your bit

With great power comes great responsibility, as the saying goes.

How are you using yours? What are you giving back to the world in which you live? How are *you* shaping it?

A few years ago, I met a woman who runs a small, local charity that supports people (mostly women) who have experienced, or are experiencing, domestic violence. She's a remarkable human being.

I spent two hours in her company the first time we met and was in tears for most of that time! I was in awe as I listened to her talk so passionately about her work and why it mattered.

As a young woman in my late teens, I was in an unhealthy, abusive relationship for a short period of time, so it didn't take much to convince me that I needed to do something to help victims of domestic violence. I came away from that meeting full of ideas, eager and excited to make a difference.

But then life got in the way. I became pregnant with my son and my priorities naturally shifted, though the urge to get involved never lessened.

It took me almost two years to act, and I wish I'd managed it sooner; in any respect, for the past two years I'm glad I've been able to give something back. In what has become an annual occurrence (and one of my favourite things to do), I organise a gift collection each Christmas for the charity in question, Pathways, and the local women's refuge, too.

It isn't a huge thing. It won't eradicate all the victims' problems or erase the charity's financial worries, but it does go some way towards helping.

The more successful I become, the more determined I become to do my bit, particularly for women. You could even say that I feel it's my duty.

At various points in my life I've needed other women to drag me to my feet when all I've wanted to do is collapse. When another woman's kind words have made all the difference on a particularly bad day, or when someone's support opened up a door of opportunity that was previously locked and bolted to me.

I honestly don't know where I would be without the women in my life that have helped me in my hour of need or been there to spur me on. To use whatever power we have to make other women feel or become more powerful **is one of the greatest things we could ever do.**

It also feels *absolutely amazing*.

'Pick Ups' To Take Away

♥ Often, society has women believing that, far from being power*ful*, they're actually power*less*. Do not let them fool you, because it's **not true**.

♥ We've become accustomed to thinking that we lack power because of the immense challenges and threats we face, due to our gender. This is why so many of us suffer feelings of powerlessness.

♥ Our daughters need to understand that they *are* powerful, regardless of what the world tries to tell them. **And so do we.**

♥ Whilst we undoubtedly face challenges we should not have to face, we also **have to take responsibility for the power we willingly hand over to others**, which leaves us vulnerable to attack.

♥ Consciously or not, many of us invite others to treat us badly; we accept things we should never allow, and we diminish our own power, every day, through our own actions.

♥ There are many ways in which we neglect or attack our power, but we are free to change these at *any* time.

♥ We cannot expect life to shower us with good fortune when we treat ourselves in ways that are detrimental to our happiness and success.

♥ We *all* have the power to create a happier future. Remember, it takes just as much power to destroy your life as it does to make it flourish.

♥ We can't control what happens to us, but even when life is at its worst, we *always* have power in the choices we make and the thoughts we create.

♥ There are lots of things you can do to feel and become more powerful, including: being courageous, changing your inner voice, and living by your own standards.

♥ If we want to thrive and realise the power we deserve, **we have to stop seeing other women as the enemy and learn to like each other again**.

♥ There's so much we can do to help one other and raise our power as a collective, such as offering our support, changing the way we behave towards one another, and giving back whenever we can.

♥ Using whatever power we may have to make other women feel or become more powerful, is one of the greatest things we can do.

REGRET

Regret

'I believe that what we regret most are our failures of courage, whether it's the courage to be kinder, to show up, to say how we feel, to set boundaries, to be good to ourselves. For that reason, regret can be the birthplace of empathy.'

~ Brene Brown

By nature, I am a leaper.

Some may say reckless, others would say impulsive, but the truth is, I like to go for things.

I've always been the kind of person who will try things out, take things a little further or experiment. Generally speaking, my inquisitive nature and determination to cram as much into this earthly experience as I can means that I tend to jump into things headfirst.

That's just who I am. Thankfully, more often than not, it's paid off, and in many cases, has even gone on to be the making of me.

However, when you're rebellious at heart, a seeker of answers, and someone who wants to do it *all,* you can often find yourself in a bit of a pickle. At times, I certainly have.

Throughout my life there have been things I've done and situations I've found myself in, which, in hindsight, I wish hadn't happened. If you were to ask me if I regretted these things, though, the answer would have to be—and could only ever be—**absolutely not.**

Many people seem to live with regret—particularly those that are advancing in their years—and this, to be totally honest, is something that terrifies me.

I never want to be that person on her deathbed who wished she'd done this or hadn't done that. I never want to get to the end of my time on Earth and regret that I didn't spend it well enough or feel that I haven't appreciated my life *or* the people in it, as much as I should have.

The very thought that people can feel this way when they come to the end of their days makes me want to weep, but it also spurs me on.

Leaping doesn't always mean I get things right. It results in occasional mistakes and my decisions are sometimes the wrong ones. But I've always thought that if I'm fortunate enough to live to be an old lady, I'd much rather have stories to tell and memories to chuckle over in my older years, than not have anything to share at all.

I'd much rather look back at my life knowing I truly lived than acknowledge, with a heavy heart, that I played it safe. So, this is what I live by.

If you want your life to count for something; if you want to be someone who has interesting, humorous, emotional and inspiring stories to tell when you're older; if you want to leave a legacy, there really is *no* other choice.

Live your life in such a way that you risk regret as much as you discourage it.

§

As a journalist in my twenties I met and interviewed many people, from the famous to the man-on-the-street.

And even though I don't get to do much interviewing these days, I still *love* to hear people's stories. In my interview for a trainee journalist position, I was asked the question: 'Why would you make a great journalist?'

My answer was easy. 'I'm nosy. Or, as I like to put it, inquisitive.'

I love learning about other people's lives as they talk. I'm genuinely interested. Keen to hear something that will allow me to see life differently, from someone else's point of view. *Everyone* has a story, or stories, that are worth sharing, even if they don't realise it. And I believe that when people know you're interested in what they have to say, they sense it and open up to you.

If you're lucky, you'll find that when someone trusts you and feels comfortable enough to share with you some of their innermost thoughts, one of two things usually happens: they either feel compelled to tell you about how they faced a personal challenge, *or* they will talk to you about something they regret.

People *long* to be vulnerable. To open up and share their thoughts, feelings, triumphs and mistakes.

It may not appear that way; people can seem guarded at first. But I know from experience that when you *do* give another person permission to speak, they'll share with you their deepest and most painful stories.

More often than not, their deepest pain will come from living with, or being haunted by, a regret.

We *all* experience regret. What matters isn't *why* we regret something, but what we do about it. In one respect, regret can be seen as a futile emotion that only serves to make us feel bad about our lives and our choices.

However, if we choose to see it differently, **it can also be a great motivator for positive change.**

I have two main trains of thought when it comes to regret: one, that it's better to regret the things I have done than the things that I haven't. And two, there's no point regretting what I've done in the past, because I can never turn the clock back.

Regret, in many ways, is just like guilt, because **it's personal to you.** Only *you* can decide what you choose to accept or heap onto your shoulders.

Some women live with regrets they shouldn't have to live with. Some women live with regrets because they're too terrified of being 'seen'. Some women live with regrets because they've measured themselves against the impossible benchmark: 'perfection'. Some women live with regrets because they're forever being made to feel bad about themselves.

Here are some regrets I hear from women on a regular basis, which I believe we should all try to put to rest—for good.

* Regretting what you've eaten

I'm going to say it. <u>Please stop feeling bad for eating delicious food.</u>

That extra piece of chocolate cake, that three-course meal last night, the fried breakfast you wolfed down the other morning after a particularly late, boozy night.

I hear women talk about their regret for eating things they 'shouldn't have', *so* often. Sadly, there's just no escaping it. It's become part of our everyday conversation.

Regretting what we've eaten is just another surefire, easy way to beat ourselves up for wrongly believing we're not good enough.

It's also an incredibly unhealthy way to think about food in general and could set us up for a disastrous relationship with the very fuel we need in order for us to survive. **Food is not our enemy.**

It's *okay* to eat foods that are high in calories. It's *okay* to indulge or eat too much of something on occasion. It's *okay* to prefer burgers to lettuce, or a chocolate hobnob to a banana.

We all know that an apple is healthier than a slab of Victoria sponge! We all know which foods are better for us. But that doesn't or shouldn't mean that we can never enjoy something delicious, decadent or something deemed 'naughty'; or, that when we do, we should immediately regret it.

It's fantastic to want to eat more healthily and I'm all for it if you're someone who's making positive improvements to your diet for the right reasons.

But can we please stop expressing regret every time we pass over a salad for pizza or take an extra cookie out of the biscuit tin to enjoy with our cup of tea?

We need to develop a less toxic, more accepting relationship with food. To eat consciously, eat well, and eat in moderation. But above all else, **we need to learn to enjoy our food and not feel bad about it!** Even when we eat the foods we're constantly told are not good for us (carbs, I'm looking at you).

Stop regretting what you eat.

Eat the cake. Don't eat the cake. Either way, don't give yourself a hard time over something that should be a pleasure.

* Regretting your new haircut

It's happened to us all. So, it's not very nice, it's just hair. It'll grow back.

* Regretting a past relationship

Please don't do this. It's utterly pointless and a total waste of energy that you could and should put to much better use.

I've had some horrible boyfriends in my time. Like, truly horrible. Men I can't actually believe I dated, now that I'm older and wiser. But I refuse to regret those relationships, as much as it would be easy for me to do so.

I once read that no love or relationship is ever wasted, and that's true. For isn't it *always* the ugliest of frogs that teaches us the most powerful lessons?

* Regretting your body shape

Women and body image. If ever there was an important topic to talk about it, it's this one. In the next chapter I'm going to explore this in much more detail, as it's something I'm incredibly passionate about. For now, I'll keep it short and sweet.

Please don't be the woman who regrets how her body looks. **Please, don't do this to yourself.**

I know women who never join in group photos or treat themselves to new clothes, because they aren't as slim as they would like to, or 'should', be.

I know women who mourn their pre-pregnancy figures—completely blind to how wonderful they look right now.

I even know some women who have stopped making the most of life, because they're so consumed by regrets with regards to their weight loss or body image.

Don't be someone who regrets how her body looks. You are a magnificent work in progress. A rare and beautiful piece of human art. **Celebrate that!**

At some points in my life I've been bigger than I am now, and I've also been smaller. I've been wobblier, and I've been more toned. My size or shape has never had any real impact on my overall happiness, confidence or success.

We must learn to appreciate how we look right now. We need to let go of any regrets, with regards to our bodies, and be grateful for the one that we have. Your body is doing an incredible job keeping you alive! Appreciate this and stop looking at your body with regretful eyes.

* **Regretting wardrobe purchases**

I don't think there will be a single reader who hasn't regretted something they've bought to wear at some point.

Jeans that were too small, or shoes that gave them blisters. A cheap suit that failed to make them feel good, or an ill-fitting dress that did 'nothing for them'.

I try and live by the rule that everything in my wardrobe must be, and needs to be, loved—even with that in mind I can still get it totally wrong. Part of the fun with fashion is trying things out, which is why this is one area of regret we can drop easily.

Try not to buy something that you don't love, which doesn't suit you, or that you cannot afford. Never buy when you're in a rush, hungover, miserable or bored. Don't spend what you haven't got and *always* try to think of longevity (not just for you, but for the planet as well).

And if you *still* make a fashion faux pas? In all honesty, come on now…so what?! In the grand scheme of things, it won't matter a jot. Give the offending item a new home: sell it and recoup some of the money you spent on it; give it to a loved one or friend who will love it or donate it to charity.

Creating your individual style isn't always easy, but it *is* supposed to be enjoyable! If regret features heavily in your wardrobe, it's time to rethink *what* you're buying and *why* you're buying it.

§

We'd all like to live a long, healthy, happy life. One filled with joy, success (however you determine this), and love. Regrets, if any, should hopefully be few and far between.

Sadly, for many people, that's not the case.

Here are some common regrets people admit to at the end of their lives, and how I believe we can best avoid them:

* **Regretting not being more loving to the people in our lives**

Give *more* love.

Be present with your loved ones and give them your undivided attention. Be there for them, as much as you can be, and appreciate them. Tell people you love them, but more importantly, make sure you show them, too.

* **Regretting not being a better spouse or parent**

What kind of spouse or parent would you like to be? What kind of spouse or parent do you wish you'd had? **Think about it, create the picture in your mind, then <u>make it happen</u>.**

How we behave in these roles is largely determined by what is demonstrated by others. If you don't like how you are or what habits you've taken on, then change them. It's never too late.

* **Regretting working too much**

We live in a society that encourages us to work harder and harder, but at what cost?

I love my job, and I truly adore what I do, but do I want to spend every minute of every day working? *Absolutely not.*

Sometimes, there's no getting away from it: we may have to work long hours, evenings or weekends. The next time you think you must work harder, or consider bringing work home to complete in your spare time, ask yourself: **can it wait? And does it *really* matter?**

We can often find ourselves working when we don't really need to, because we feel we *should*, or that it's expected of us. Be honest with yourself, and don't ever feel bad for relaxing and enjoying your life. No one is here to work themselves to death.

* Regretting not taking more risks

I've mentioned this earlier: there's only one way to tackle this. Become **a leaper.**

You'll gain nothing from playing it safe. Not even personal comfort. Every time you turn down an opportunity that has your heart screaming 'yes!'; every time you stop yourself trying new things or stepping out of your comfort zone, you'll forever be haunted by regret for not taking more risks.

You were not created to play things safe.

Learn how to leap and take comfort in the fact that, even if something doesn't work out, at least you'll know you gave it a shot.

* Regretting not being happier or enjoying life more

Much of the time, we look for happiness in the wrong places. In new clothes, the bottom of a bottle, or our Instagram likes. We think happiness is out there, just waiting to be found, when actually it's already within us.

The choice to be happy—or not—is yours. Somebody, I can't remember who, said that to me a few years ago and it took me ages to get my head around it at first.

Perhaps I didn't want to believe it, but it's true. In my experience, it seems to boil down to two things: gratitude for *everything* you have in your life now, and to live in the present. When I make an effort to do both, my happiness levels soar.

* Regretting not going for your dreams

Some people don't go for their dreams because they tell themselves the wrong stories. They tell themselves they're too old or too poor. Too educated or not educated enough. That they haven't got the money, the talent or the time. And they believe it.

But this is just fear talking.

Our dreams are there for the taking, but we have to believe this in order to fight the fear and unravel all the negative stories we've told ourselves (probably for years).

Take this book, for instance. It's been a dream of mine since childhood and here I am, almost near the end—scared and anxious. I haven't slept properly in weeks but, still, I'm going for it.

Our dreams can indeed come to life, but we must show some serious mettle and determination first to make them happen.

* Regretting not taking better care of yourself.

This one is such an easy regret to put right. Most of us, in my experience, are dreadful at taking care of ourselves, particularly mothers. I totally get this. We're so busy looking after other people and running our lives, that it can often feel impossible to take better care of ourselves.

I assure you it's not. I also promise that when you *do* take better care of yourself, you will want to do a whole lot more of it.

Start small (because it's easier and quicker). And do *not* feel guilty.

Here are some things you can do in the name of self-care... Book yourself in for that overdue haircut or go to bed thirty minutes earlier. Take a daily multi-vitamin, or swap cups of coffee for glasses of water. Set up a savings account and put money into it every month, even if it's only a tiny amount. Give away any clothes that make you feel less than your best or treat yourself to a new lipstick. Book yourself in for that smear test or take a weekly exercise class.

And the big one? **Stop allowing people to treat you badly, whoever they are.**

One healthy new habit leads to bigger, healthier new habits, so start today. We *all* should learn to take better care of ourselves.

* Regretting not doing more for others

Many people wrongly believe that they have little influence on the lives of others. This is simply not true. We *all* have the ability to make or ruin someone else's day, as we go about our business.

Let me give you an example. When I worked as a journalist, I did a job swap that saw me go from working on magazines to doing a stint on my local newspaper, in order to gain new skills and boost my journalistic experience.

For six weeks, I worked in a new environment with a bunch of people I didn't know, doing a job that was very different to the one I'd been doing.

Every day I'd walk into the big, open plan office and say 'good morning' to the journalists there. If I was lucky, one or two of them would acknowledge my presence and perhaps even look up. Most people, however, were unwelcoming.

Thankfully, one guy, who worked in the sports section, would always repeat my 'good morning' and give me a smile. One guy made this new—and, in many ways, daunting—experience much easier to bear. Without his warmth and friendliness, my time on the newspaper would have been a less enjoyable experience. Tellingly, I still think of him fondly even today, unlike many of the other journalists whose names I can't even remember.

We all can, and should, do more to help each other. This does not have to be in impossible or unmanageable ways. It doesn't even have to cost time or money. We can all help to make the world a better place, in our own way, simply by being kinder and by looking out for each other.

A smile. A compliment. A helping hand. They all go a long way to brightening someone's day or making an impact. Never underestimate the power you have to change someone's day or life.

* Regretting not choosing more meaningful work

I was thirty when I decided to quit my job as a marketing manager and work for myself.

It was one of the boldest things I've ever done and remains one of my best decisions. And not just because of my professional development and the exciting opportunities that have arisen as a result, but because I get to spend my days doing exactly what I love. I *never* have that 'back to work' feeling.

I've worked all kinds of jobs in the past that I haven't loved, just to earn money. I'd go back to them all in a heartbeat, if I needed to earn more to feed my children or put clothes on their backs. I'm aware that we're all doing the best we can to survive, financially or otherwise.

But, if you do hate your job, I would just like to say this: **don't ever settle or think it's your only option.** It may not seem like it, but I promise you, from my own experience, **doors of opportunity will present themselves if you seek them out**. If you're courageous enough to take a gamble and try something new.

We spend so much of our time at work. Most of our lives, in fact, which is *way* too much time to spend doing something we don't love, doing something that doesn't make us happy or which we don't perceive to be meaningful.

It's *never* too late to change job or career.

* Regretting not speaking up more

How many times have you kicked yourself for not speaking up?

Certainly, in my life, there have been a number of times when I've regretted not being more courageous or not saying what I needed to say at the time. When I wished I'd said 'sorry' and 'I love you' more or regretted not explaining my actions better. When I've wished I'd told people why I hold them dear or said kinder things to people when they needed to hear them.

It can take real courage to speak up. To tell someone the truth or to find the right words to say. To ask for what we deserve or to defend others when they're being attacked.

It's not always easy. Women are not encouraged to speak up and speak out.

We need to get better at this. If we want to live an authentic life with few regrets, we must own our voice and use it in the best way we can.

§

Here are some tactics I use to get me through life, whilst collecting as few regrets as I possibly can:

* I go with my gut instinct

I once saw a psychic medium who told me, 'Katie, you have incredible instincts, but you ignore them far too often, at your own peril.'

I had to laugh—never had a truer word been spoken!

It's taken me decades to trust my instincts. I'm so much better at listening to them now than I used to be. These days, whether it involves people, food, situations or opportunities, if I sense something is 'off'', I listen. And if my instincts tell me to go for something, I jump as high as I can.

* I imagine the future and consider if the issue that appears to matter now will matter then

Since having Leo, I've had to pull back on my workload; I just don't have as much time to dedicate to my career at the moment as I'd like.

Sometimes, this has been hard to accept. I've often had to be stern with myself and ask: 'What will I regret more when I'm older? Spending less time with my children or not working hard enough?'

For me, the answer is simple. I've therefore stepped back a little from my work so I can be a mum who's around more for her kids.

Granted, it's a choice that may not be for everyone. But it's *my* best choice because it's important to me. Next time you find yourself struggling to decide what to do, ask yourself: **will it matter in years to come?**

* I do my best to give back

Our legacy. In other words, what we'll leave when we're gone from this world.

I try to ensure that what I leave behind will be something worth leaving. It's why I strive to give back. I try to help others and be a good person as much as I possibly can.

* I try to slow down and appreciate things

Admittedly, I don't always manage this, but whenever and wherever possible I take a step back to appreciate life from where I stand.

Kids are the best teachers in this regard. When I watch my two children playing or drawing, when I see them collapse in squeals of laughter or run around the house without a care in the world, I'm reminded that life isn't just about *doing*.

It's also about *being* and making the best of any given moment.

* **I ask myself: 'Will I regret this in the future if I don't go for it?'**

If the answer is no, I leave things alone. But, if the answer is yes, I'll do my best to ignore my fearful brain, and instead, focus on facing whatever is making me feel scared or nervous.

* **If it's not an easy yes, then it's a no**

What we say yes or no to *matters*. From helping people to trying out new things, to spending money to working with a client. If my immediate reaction isn't a big, fat, happy 'yes!' then it's a definite 'no'.

* **I value experiences more than material things**

Last year my husband and I chose to spend a huge chunk of our savings on a month-long trip to Australia instead of installing a new bathroom.

Some people may think we were crazy. It was just common sense to us.

As expected, the holiday turned out to be the trip of a lifetime for our family and one that we'll never forget. It's hard to go wrong when spending money on experiences, which is why I'll always choose them over material possessions.

* **I think to myself, 'Will I be proud of myself for doing this? Will others be proud of me?'**

When it comes to opportunities and challenges, for me, this one is really important.

If it's not going to benefit me and make me feel good about myself or make those who know me feel good in some way, too, I'm not interested.

For instance, I have huge hopes for this book. More than I dare think about. Regardless of how many copies it sells or how many people it reaches, what I know is this: I will always be proud of myself for creating it and seeing it through to the end. Anything else that comes my way as a result will only be the icing on the cake.

* I try to look after myself

In all areas of my life—physically, mentally, spiritually and financially—I try and look after myself as best I can. I know that I deserve my own kindness and care. (And so, my friend, do you.)

None of us know how long we'll inhabit the Earth, or how many more times we will walk with our loved ones, gaze at the stars or feel the air in our lungs.

Life is miraculous. Giving birth twice made me realise this. The safe delivery of both my children made me appreciate how miraculous we all are, and also how robust yet incredibly fragile our earthly existence truly is.

It's easy to forget this when we're busy simply getting through each day. Stuck in cycles of working and parenting, and *doing, doing, doing*. Weeks whizz by, months come and go; before we know it our children will have left home and we'll be facing a new chapter.

We cannot allow our lives to merely pass us by. We must craft them into lives that we love and which we're proud of. We must create our own stories to ensure they're ones worth telling.

Because the biggest regret we *all* face—more than *any* other—is that we'll have wasted our limited time here.

That we never really lived.

'Pick Ups' To Take Away

♥ If you want your life to count for something, you must live it in such a way that you risk welcoming regret as much as you discourage it.

♥ Often, somebody's deepest pain comes from living with, or being haunted by, a regret.

♥ Regret, if we choose to see it differently, **can be a great motivator for positive change.**

♥ Regret, in many ways, is just like guilt, because **it's personal to you.** Only *you* can decide what you choose to accept or heap onto your shoulders.

♥ Do your best to let go of the regrets that, as women, we've been told we should have. Never regret eating certain foods, past relationships or how your body looks.

♥ Don't let a lifetime of regrets be your future. Think of the most common regrets people have at the end of their lives and do your best to avoid them. Show yourself and others more love and kindness, demonstrate greater courage, and aim to leave a wonderful legacy. Reduce the time spent thinking of work, fuelling fear, or just beating yourself up.

♥ Use some of my tactics—or create your own—to help you live your best life, with as few regrets as possible. Things that help me include trusting my instincts, thinking about how I may feel in the future, doing my best to give back, and making an effort to continually challenge myself.

♥ Your life is precious, so don't let it pass you by. Respect it and shape it into a life that you adore and which you can be proud of. **Create your own story.**

♥ The biggest regret we all face is the thought that we've wasted our limited time here and that **we didn't really live.**

~~HATE~~

Love

Love

As women, we walk the miserable path of self-hatred too often and far too easily. In many ways, it's not our fault.

Conditioned from a young age to dislike who we are and how we look, we've been actively encouraged to despise ourselves by society and the world at large and have therefore become good at it.

Self-hatred has become our default button. And when it comes to other women…well, we've done a pretty good job at hating one another, too.

It's easy for us, and also depressingly normal.

It doesn't have to be this way.

We live in an age that makes it easier for us to speak out and share our stories and opinions. The internet may have many faults, but it has also given women the power to use their voices as they see fit, to such an extent that we've never seen before. Some very fortunate women, like me, are even able to make a career out of it.

No longer do we need to gain approval from an editor to have our work published or to share our thoughts. We can pop onto one of our social media channels or publish a blog post to say whatever it is we have to say. We're able to share it with many others in an instant.

If handled well, this is incredibly empowering. The

power that lies in our hands, thanks to the internet, should never be underestimated. Because everything we share—indeed, everything we talk about—**has the potential to shift us towards a path of acceptance and self-love.**

It's not going to be easy. Though there's plenty of positive noise and activity in the online world, the internet is also the perfect arena for those who wish to keep us stuck in a cycle of self-hatred.

It's why you find celebrities peddling awful dieting products to their impressionable (and often, incredibly young) followers for a heap of cash. It's why thousands of photo-editing apps have been created, which enable you to change how you look in images in a matter of seconds. It's why famous women edit their photographs, slimming their bodies down to look a size or two smaller than they actually are in real life, even if they deny that they do this.

Amongst all the filters, lies and self-hatred, though, it's possible to find content online that will make your heart swell and your inner lioness roar.

When I hear women accept their body shape; when I come across a video of a woman in her seventies attending New York Fashion Week…it gives me hope that our future as women *can* be much brighter—and happier, too.

Loving ourselves for who we are and for whatever unique contribution we can bring to the world is <u>not</u> an impossible dream!

It actually takes a lot of energy to hate ourselves, and one another. Just imagine how incredible our lives could become if we took that energy and channelled it towards something more positive.

Imagine if we flipped our negative emotions, thoughts and beliefs, and transformed them into healthier ones. I believe the world would be our oyster.

It's not easy to love ourselves when we're forever told we're not good enough. It's difficult to believe our individual worth and greatness when, throughout our lives, we've been told, shown and actively encouraged to believe our voices, opinions, talents and feelings don't *really* matter. Or, certainly not as much as those of the opposite sex. Our worth is often limited and measured.

Be nice.

Look pretty.

Stay young.

This is what we're told will give us worth in the world and yet it couldn't be more wrong. I think we all know this deep down. We know we can and *do* offer so much more than this, but somehow, we still believe the lies and fall in with the crowd. We try hard to be nice, look pretty and stay young. We do our best to please everyone, and spend a small fortune on our appearance, fighting any signs of ageing with all the aggression we can muster.

Not because *we* don't know what we're worth, but because we're terrified that our worth will be ignored, overlooked or forgotten by others.

Everywhere we turn, billboards, magazine covers and television adverts scream their messages of self-improvement—telling us to change and spend money, suggesting that only then will we become loveable.

Which is perhaps why so many of us mistakenly believe we can find happiness or satisfaction in a pot of miracle cream, a smaller dress size, or a vial of Botox.

It's why so many of us have spent more than we can afford, made more effort than we perhaps should have, and why we ferociously fight our weight and age.

But, none of this stuff works—at least, not in the long term. If it did, why would there be so many women walking around today who *still* don't like themselves?

Why would there be so many women out there who cannot bear to look at themselves naked in the mirror?

Why would so many women be bitter about getting older, when it's a gift denied to some?

Spending money. Fighting our bodies. Trying to look how we did at thirty when we turn fifty.

None of the potions, creams or similar 'miracles' cure the self-hatred women can feel. In fact, in most cases, they only serve to amplify it.

The *only* cure that will make us happier is learning to love who we truly are.

The term 'self-love' is bandied about a lot these days. So much so, it's in danger of losing its importance, of being mocked or totally disregarded.

Yet learning to love yourself is *the* best, and most important, thing you can ever do for yourself.

Because everything, absolutely *everything*, stems from this.

You'll no doubt have heard people say this or come across quotes to this effect on social media. It sounds trite, doesn't it, when people say loving yourself is the key to *everything?*

If you've ever tried to love yourself, though, you'll know how difficult it is to achieve. Learning to love ourselves—and I believe, for most of us, it is a case of *learning* how to do so—can be a real struggle.

And maintaining self-love is an endless, uphill battle, because of the toxic messages we receive throughout our lives. Loving ourselves is a battle that you and I will forever have to fight.

But it's one that's worth the effort. Without self-love we'll never be as happy as we deserve to be or understand how incredible we truly are.

We'll never rise to the levels of success we may hope to achieve or experience all the wonders life can offer. If we don't love ourselves, we'll never be treated in the way we deserve to be, nor learn how to treat others in the way they deserve, too.

Without self-love, life can feel daunting, miserable, painful and mediocre. Yet, with self-love, everything feels possible and the personal challenges we all experience from time to time become easier to bear.

I'm telling you this, not because I've read about it— or even because I believe it; I've learned from personal experience that it's **the truth.**

Throughout my teens, I had little self-esteem. Truth be told, I'm not sure I even knew what self-esteem meant. I certainly didn't love who I was.

But what I did know, what I could recognise even as a teenager, was that deep down I felt something was missing. There was a feeling of emptiness inside me that I just couldn't fill.

I'd watch my close friends with envy as they approached situations with a confidence I didn't have. I'd marvel at how easily they defended themselves against others and how unashamedly they'd express their feelings. I'd wonder, 'What on earth is wrong with me? Why can't I do that!?' I didn't understand, as I do now, that it was because I didn't love myself. Or that my core central belief was that I wasn't worthy or good enough.

So, I spent my teenage years hiding away, coasting and failing. I treated myself appallingly and allowed others to do the same.

I didn't put myself forward for things. I didn't try my best. I didn't speak up for myself. I didn't speak up for others. I was unkind to myself (although I didn't realise that at the time); perhaps unsurprisingly other people were unkind to me, too. And I accepted this.

I didn't understand why my behaviour was different to that of my peers and closest friends. I couldn't understand why I admired my best friend's older (and incredibly confident and self-assured) sister so much.

I just didn't get it. But I *did* know there was something very wrong. In my late teens, any scrap of self-esteem and love I'd managed to hold onto throughout those challenging years was soon left in tatters when I began a relationship with an older man who treated me badly.

It was a toxic, abusive relationship and it took me to a dark, lonely place.

Loving someone who claims to adore you but whose actions appear to come from a place of hatred does a lot more than mess with your mind. It messes with your soul.

At eighteen years old, during a time in my life when I should have felt excited, happy and optimistic for the future, I instead felt utterly worthless.

When the relationship (thankfully) ended eighteen months later, I was left a sad, confused, broken young woman.

I did what any sad, confused, broken young person would do: I began to self-destruct. And I did a *really* good job at it.

I couldn't comprehend any of this back then, of course. I thought my experience was normal. I thought *I* was normal and that was just how life was.

As I sit here, at thirty-nine years of age and living a life I absolutely love, I'm not sure which is more painful to accept: that I thought, back then, I was okay and that what happened was the 'norm', or that I didn't realise life could be *so* much better.

That time in my life is not one I look back on fondly. It can make me feel embarrassed, shameful, sad and disappointed, if I allow it to, yet it's not all doom and gloom. Yes, my late teenage years were awful to experience, but they also proved a blessing of sorts. Because it was only when I hit the self-destruct button and watched my life as I knew it burn to the ground, that the desire within me to create a better, happier life was ignited.

My feisty side saved me; it wouldn't allow me to give up on myself. I made the decision to take myself from a place of total self-hatred to one of self-love—and I've remained on that journey for twenty years now.

It's been a *long* process. Two decades of continuous effort, self-reflection, determination and questioning, to repair the young, broken Katie.

I feel like I've done it, though. Today, with grit, grimace, mistakes aplenty, and a hell of a lot of reading and prayer, I am finally able to say that I love myself.

I honestly can't tell you how bloody marvellous it feels, or how much I long for other women to feel the same.

§

'She loves herself.'

How many times have you heard or even said this about another woman, in negative tones?

In the back of my mind as I write this, I cannot escape the irony…that whilst I'm doing my best to encourage you all to do better at self-love, the phrase 'she loves herself' is still seen as an insult.

Why?!

Why do people feel threatened when they come across

a woman who actually likes who she is? Is it because it goes against the norm of most women hating themselves? Is it jealousy, because we wish we had an ounce of her confidence, charisma and self-assurance?

Why do we say this when we want to bring a woman down a peg or two? When we think she's 'too big for her boots'?

Whatever the reason, and I'm sure there are many more, we must stop seeing women loving themselves as a bad thing and start seeing it as **something we should all be aiming for!**

Wouldn't it be fantastic if the only time the words 'she loves herself' are muttered in the future is when someone wants to give a woman a massive compliment, instead of attempting to pull her down? We can make that happen, starting today!

It's *good* to see women who love themselves. There are not enough of us in this world. We need more role models of this kind for women today, as well as for future generations.

Self-love, whilst empowering, is also incredibly fragile, so let's stop hurling the phrase 'she loves herself' around as an insult and start supporting more of this instead.

If you *are* someone who feels the need to say it about another woman, because you're threatened by their high levels of self-esteem and self-worth, please, do yourself a favour and see this as a big, red flag to do some work on those areas within you.

Perhaps talk of self-love makes you feel uncomfortable because you don't like yourself very much. Maybe you recognise that you have a lot of inner work to do.

If so…congratulations! Welcome to my club! Seriously, this self-love malarkey never ends. We're *all* a work in progress.

I'm going to share with you some of the things that have helped me to like myself much more. How you choose to boost the love you have for yourself will be a personal thing; however, you might wish to consider some of these options.

At times it won't be easy. You'll probably find, like I did and still do from time to time, when your guard is down, you'll end up slipping back into old patterns. The negative chatter in your mind may rear its ugly voice once again.

Don't give up! Because little by little, you *will* move towards a much happier, confident, increasingly-loving and self-assured place.

Work you do on yourself in this area will only help *change your life for the better*.

* I read everything to do with self-help

Okay, maybe I'm exaggerating a little. I haven't read *everything* on the subject of self-help, but I have read an awful lot of self-improvement books over the past two decades, and what I can tell you is this: they help, a *lot*.

I know—and no doubt you will, too—some people who think it's pathetic or weak to read self-development books. But, if you want my advice, you'll ignore everything they have to say on the matter and instead head over to the self-help aisle of your nearest library or book shop as soon as possible.

Admittedly, there are some rubbish examples out there, and you may feel some titles are not for you. But there are loads by brilliant people that will change the way you think and help you improve your life. Let the wise words of others soak into your psyche and lead you down a more positive path.

If you don't believe how powerful a book can be, let me tell you about one in particular that changed my life around nine years ago. The incredible **Linchpin**, by Seth Godin, was handed to me by my husband to read, after he became tired of hearing me whine on a daily basis about my job as a marketing manager for an educational tech firm.

'Here, try this,' he said, tossing me the book. I read it across two evenings, and the day after I'd finished reading it, I handed in my notice to go freelance.

It remains one of the boldest moves I've ever made and also one of the best. It's all thanks to that book and Seth's incredible wisdom.

* I started to question my beliefs

I cannot emphasise enough how important this is or how essential it will be to your personal growth.

Questioning your beliefs and stories is one of the best ways to unravel your thinking and turn things around. Next time you find yourself being critical with yourself, when you judge another person or hate the world at large, take a moment and ask yourself, 'Where has this belief come from?' And then, 'Is it true?'

Many of us—including me—even carry around beliefs that are not our own. Some we will have picked up in childhood. Others will have come from our peers. Many we have inherited from the society in which we live.

Some beliefs may have served us well in the past but are no longer needed today. Others will have crept up on us without us even realising.

Question what you believe to be true, especially when it comes to how you think or feel about yourself.

Whatever you *believe* to be true <u>becomes</u> your truth, whether you like it or not.

* I make an effort to like myself

It's as simple and as difficult as that!

I constantly choose to like who I am. I constantly choose to see the good in me. I constantly choose to be kinder to myself.

I don't always manage it. I wish I could tell you it's a breeze, but it's not. I still have days when I berate myself or only see faults when I look in the mirror. Every day, I try my damnedest to like and accept who I am. Wrinkles, cellulite, bad tempers, occasional negative attitude and all.

* I'm choosier about who I allow in my life

I was not always this way. In the past, I've allowed my kind, 'see the good in all' nature to override my instincts and have been badly burnt on many an occasion as a result. I've been a dreadful judge of character over the years (unlike my husband who's brilliant at sussing people out).

Here's something to inspire you: I'm getting *so* much better at it.

Be very careful about who you allow in your life. Consider other people's motives; pay close attention to their behaviour and actions and much less to their words.

Somebody once said to me, **'Not everyone who appears to be your friend, is your friend.'** Sadly, this is true.

People can masquerade as your friend. They can appear to like you or say that they do. They may compliment you and be eager to spend time with you. But watch out for the signs.

Watch out for anyone who throws little digs in your direction. Anyone who isn't there for you in your hour of need. Anyone who cannot celebrate your happiness or success. Anyone who takes from you but never gives.

Anyone who puts you down, drains you of energy or treats you poorly… they are **not** your friend.

We become the people we surround ourselves with. I cannot stress this enough.

When it comes to your inner circle, choose wisely! Do not tolerate anyone in your life who makes you feel bad or 'less than'.

You're an adult now, and you can choose.

Every time you allow someone to treat you appallingly, you're basically handing them a sledgehammer and asking them to aim a blow at your fragile self-esteem. You also, unwittingly, encourage more awful behaviour from others, because they know you will accept it.

* **When I look at myself in the mirror, I say kind things**

It sounds a little bit silly, granted, but it works. After giving birth to my second child, I knew from experience that my body was going to look a bit battered, bruised, swollen and marked for some time.

I didn't just accept this fact, **I made a point of appreciating it**. I refuse to be critical of my appearance and body in any way—particularly when I'm at my most vulnerable. For me, actively trying to only say kind things to myself has worked wonders over the years.

We are our own harshest critics, but **we must learn to be our own best friends.** Say kind things to yourself. Change your inner dialogue. Focus only on the parts of you that you like, and if nothing else, try this: every time you see your reflection, say to yourself 'I AM enough.'

Do this often and it won't be long before it becomes your new truth.

* **I try to make time for *me***

I recognise that, for most of us, spending any time on

ourselves, when there are a-million-and-one other things we could be doing, can feel strange. Alien, even.

But you must give yourself permission to reboot and relax. The only person who can look after your mental health and wellbeing is *you,* so make sure you do a decent job of it and find a way to give yourself time off from doing, doing, doing—whenever you need to—so that you can just 'be'.

* I don't give what I don't have

There's a wise saying: *you cannot pour from an empty cup*. Very true.

In the past, on many occasions, I've foolishly given more of myself than I actually had to give. More than was expected of me, in some cases.

Time. Money. Energy. Kindness. Expertise. Skills.

Situations where I chose to give away my resources so others could benefit, even though doing so proved detrimental to myself.

Giving more than you can afford to give, reinforces the toxic belief that you are *not* worthy. It demonstrates that you think other people are worthier of what you have to offer than you! Only give what you can afford to give.

* I challenge myself

As much as I can, and I swear by it. Nothing is greater for building confidence than when you take yourself out of your comfort zone and do something completely new or terrifying.

Learn to fight the fear and push yourself as much as possible. It gets easier the more you do it.

* I don't allow the opinions of others to become *my* truth

Other people's opinions of you should *not* matter to you more than your own, so please don't allow them to.

How other people react to us. How other people treat us. How other people see us…is to do with *their* issues.

None of us can control what somebody else thinks or feels about us, which is why people-pleasing never works. We can, however, control which words or opinions to accept or 'let in'. Don't allow the words or opinions of others to taint your opinion of, or belief in, yourself.

* I invest in myself

People who like themselves are good at investing in themselves, **because they know they deserve it.** Take a leaf out of their book and do the same. The more I invest in myself, the better I feel—and the more other people are willing to invest in me, too.

* I try not to take myself too seriously

When your self-esteem is fragile, like mine was years ago, it's almost impossible to accept feedback (no matter how constructive) or be able to laugh at yourself.

Your delicate ego can't deal with any perceived criticism or slight. As my self-esteem and confidence grew, I found I was more able to laugh at myself when things went wrong or when I messed up. It's such a relief!

Try not to take yourself too seriously. Take things with a pinch of salt where possible, and laugh when you make a mistake, as much as you can. We're all just winging our way through life on a hope and a prayer.

* I try to present my best self

My mum has always made an effort with how she looks and what she wears.

I can count on two hands the amount of times I've seen her without make-up or looking bedraggled, and I'm grateful to her that she instilled in me the notion that it's important to present your best physical self to the world.

This doesn't mean I dress up every day or that I won't leave the house without a full face of make-up (although, if you see me without mascara, you'll know something is very, very wrong!), but it does mean that I care about my appearance and that I always try to look clean, stylish and relatively pulled together.

Do I do this for other people? Yes. More importantly, though, I do it for **me**, because it makes me feel good.

* I ask for what I believe I deserve

If you don't ask, you don't get. This is probably my top tip that I'd give to anyone, particularly if they work for themselves or they want to forge their way in a creative field.

I used to be terrified of asking for anything and I could kick myself now for the times I never asked for a pay rise when I knew I deserved one, or when I needed some help with something but was too embarrassed to ask for it.

Freelancing changed all of that for me. I soon realised that, unless I reached out to people, things wouldn't happen, the work wouldn't always come, and I'd risk not being paid.

In my experience, most people want to help, and enjoy helping, other people. Make yourself a promise that, from now on, you'll do your best to ask for what you deserve.

The worst anyone can say to you is 'no'. That's okay—if I can deal with an occasional no, so can you. But trust me, more often than not, you'll be astonished at how many times people actually say yes.

* I try to be a decent human being

It's not a coincidence that hurt people go on to hurt others. So, be good. Be kind. Be thoughtful. And be genuine, for it's impossible to have a true liking, love and respect for yourself if you don't behave like a decent human being.

§

Finally, I cannot leave this chapter or bring this book to a close before talking about the thing most women seem to find hard to love about themselves—an issue more difficult than any other.

Their bodies.

Learning to love our bodies is one of our biggest challenges as a female. We've become obsessed with our size, ashamed of our curves, and terrified of getting bigger.

Day after day, I hear women talking about how they need to lose weight, tone up or get back in their pre-pregnancy skinny jeans. They lament over how much they've eaten for lunch or celebrate how 'good' they've been.

Reaching for a magazine in the hairdressers, I felt angry when I saw famous women being lambasted on the cover for piling on the pounds. If I pop onto social media I'll come across various women sharing how much weight they've lost and being congratulated for it.

It makes me sad, angry, and incredibly disappointed.

Amongst my friends and most of the women I know, in some ways I'm a bit of an odd one. I rarely, if ever, talk about my weight, what I've eaten or weight loss. I don't do diets. I don't believe in not eating certain things.

And I never congratulate my friends if they lose weight. Not because I'm heartless, but because, to me, they're *always* beautiful and no dress size—bigger or smaller—will ever change that.

Giving women praise for becoming slimmer puts us all on shaky ground and threatens already-fragile self-esteem, which is why I'm loath to do it.

I never comment on someone's body shape or ask them if they've lost weight, and I try not to get into conversations about this kind of thing at all. It's unhealthy, it's damaging, and also because we have *so* much more we should be talking about, worrying about, and paying attention to than this.

My body is far from perfect.

It's been through two pregnancies and given birth twice. It's breastfed both my children and it's aged, too. It's not the same as it once was; it's not as lean or toned.

Thanks to pregnancy, I've acquired a few stretch marks and a squishy bit at the bottom of my tummy that will never go back to how it used to be. But when I look in the mirror, I *am* proud of what I see. My curves and feminine shape. The marks that came from carrying my children. A body that has enjoyed so many pleasures in life—from delicious food to hot sex, from swimming in the ocean to dancing on tables. I see a body that has given me the greatest gift: becoming a parent, twice over. A body that may look different to how it did years ago, but a body that's marvellous all the same.

I'm a woman who's grown more comfortable in her skin the older I've become. I'm a woman who loves her body, even the imperfect, wobbly bits.

I realise how fortunate I am to see myself this way, when so many women don't, or simply can't. Looking back, I guess I've always been happy with my body. Even as a teen, when a few boys in my class would call me 'ironing board' due to my (then) flat chest. Even when certain women have made me question how I look.

For those of you that struggle to love your body, here are some things I do on a regular basis that have enabled me to maintain a healthy, happy body image:

* I try not to compare

One of my best friends at college had *the* most amazing legs. The kind of legs you'd see in a magazine. My legs are one of my best features, yet hers 'knocked mine out of the park'.

Did I mind? No! I still loved my legs, even though hers were much more beautiful.

If you continually measure your body against others, you will fail, which is why you must concentrate on *you.*

Perhaps you have the softest skin or eyes that can melt the toughest of hearts. Maybe you hate your tummy, yet your waist is magnificently small. **Whichever part of your body you feel is the best, concentrate on that and stop comparing any part of yourself with that of others.**

* I try to appreciate it

I did everything to avoid stretch marks when I was pregnant, so I was rather dismayed when they started to pop up from nowhere in my last trimester. I admit that I wasn't too keen on them at first. Now, years later, I forget they're even there. When I am reminded of them, I run my fingers over the faint, silvery streaks and send them some love.

We must learn to appreciate our bodies, *especially* the bits we don't particularly like.

* I focus on the positive

Some women will avoid seeing themselves naked. If you're one of them, I urge you to change your perception.

In those first few weeks after Elsie was born, my body looked like nothing I'd ever seen before. It was a little horrifying, truth be told. I still faced the mirror whilst naked, though, and tried my best to like what I saw.

Look at your body and find something positive to say

about it. I guarantee that you'll start to feel happier about how you look if you change *your* perception.

* I listen to those who love me

My husband has always been, and continues to be, my body's greatest fan. I'm well aware how fortunate I am to be with a man who only ever sees my beauty.

Listen to the people you love, and who love you, when they say nice things about your shape. When your husband tells you that you're beautiful, believe him! When your best friend tells you that you have the most sensational figure, believe *her*!

Women have a tendency to tune out all the good stuff people say about them and instead focus on the bad. If you learn how to accept a compliment, it can really help the way you feel about yourself.

* I don't buy or read any magazine that promotes weight loss, or which makes women feel bad about their size

You know the ones I'm talking about. The weeklies or monthlies that feature unflattering images of famous woman on their covers and encourage us to join in with their criticism. The ones that tell you how to lose half a stone in three days on their (crazy) detox plan.

They're not nice. They won't make you feel good about yourself. *And* they promote hate. Stop buying and reading them.

* I try to eat well and exercise

I do neither of these as much as I *should,* but I do know this: whenever I eat healthier foods and move around a bit more, I always look and feel better.

I don't do diets, nor do I believe in excessive working out; however, I *do* believe in looking after yourself wherever and whenever possible.

* I'm realistic

Would I love to be as shapely as Jennifer Lopez? Hell, yes! But I've accepted that this will never happen because my body isn't the same as hers. I focus on **what I *have* got instead. I focus on my body and its uniqueness.**

We're not all meant to be the same size or shape. Some women are naturally slim. Others look fabulous with curves, and there are hundreds more shapes and sizes in and around these, too. The key to being happier with your body is working out what feels right for you, and learning to see and appreciate *your* body for exactly what it is.

§

A few years ago, as I walked down the street, I caught a snippet of a conversation between a mum and her young daughter. It took my breath away. It appeared to be just general chit-chat.

The girl said to her mum, *'I'm so excited for dinner. I can't wait to have fish and chips.'*

The mother replied, 'That's great, darling, Mummy's hungry, too. I must go on a diet tomorrow, though; I can't have too many chips as they'll make me fat.'

The girl, who was probably about seven years of age, looked a little confused for a moment then she nodded her head. They strode off, hand in hand.

It wasn't an extraordinary conversation, but that moment forever changed how I talk about my body and how I view it.

Since that day, I've never talked about my body in negative terms in front of my daughter, or anyone else. And should Elsie catch me walking around the bedroom naked, I make sure I walk proudly, with my head held high.

Since that day, I've refused to feel guilty if I fancy a Big Mac every now and then, or if I drink too much wine on a rare occasion.

I'm so *tired* of hearing women say dreadful things about their bodies. And I'm so angry that a culture of shame, negativity and criticism has been allowed to grow. Our relationships with our incredible bodies are complex. We grow babies, we change shape, we get fitter, we get fatter, we get thinner, we get older. And throughout all this, the world watches.

Models are photoshopped to impossible standards yet held up as the physical ideal. We're told not to get too large but we're similarly lambasted if deemed too thin.

Our pregnant bumps are commented on and seen as public property. Our breasts are either admired or seen as offensive. We're told what we can and can't wear to cover up our bodies.

The fallout of this sees us punishing our bodies by starving ourselves or eating too much. We veer from showing off our bodies as trophies and covering them up because we're ashamed. We reshape them with cosmetic surgery or stop caring about how our bodies look altogether.

We become jealous of other women that we think look better than us. And we absolutely dread getting older. We punish and criticise our bodies, the cycle of hatred propelling itself effortlessly from one generation of women to the next.

When did we start thinking of our bodies as our enemy? And why on Earth have we allowed this to happen? Our imperfect-but-perfectly-functioning, life-giving bodies do *not* deserve this. They don't deserve the awful things we say about them. They don't deserve to be viewed through critical eyes. We may struggle to love our bodies, yet they continue to love, nurture and support us. Keeping us alive. Creating future generations. Breathing. Moving. Birthing babies. Giving pleasure. Isn't it time we showed them more respect? Isn't it time we spoke about them more positively?

If *we* do not learn to love our bodies, we will <u>never</u> claim them back from a society that wants us to hate them.

If *we* do not learn to love our bodies, our daughters will never learn to love theirs.

We must start loving our bodies and celebrating them, not because they're perfect, but because they're wonderfully, beautifully *imperfect,* and because they're *ours!*

I long for the day when mothers teach their young daughters that a woman's body is not something to be at war with.

I long for the day when the beautiful women I know recognise their beauty. I long for the day when no one feels any guilt for tucking into a few chips.

Please, love your body if you don't already. Appreciate how fabulous it is and stop berating it for not living up to an impossible ideal.

Stop trying to be the 'ideal size' and focus your attention on creating a fuller, happier life instead. This will bring you more happiness and satisfaction than the weighing scales ever can.

§

From hating myself as a teenager on the cusp of womanhood to loving myself as a woman in the last year of her thirties, no one is more shocked than me as to how far I've come.

My life could have been very different if I'd chosen to settle. If I hadn't picked myself up. If I hadn't dug deep and found some serious mettle when it was required.

Today I live a full, happy life, doing work that I love and with a family I adore. It isn't perfect. Nobody's life is.

There are areas that need work and things I'd like to change, but it's a life I've created on my own terms, together with the most wonderful partner...my love, my rock, and my best friend.

Did I ever imagine my life could be so fabulous and fulfilling? Did I ever imagine my career could be so exciting? Absolutely not. This is what happens when you begin to love yourself and realise your own worth. **Life opens up and surprises you.**

Doors unexpectedly open, magic starts to happen, and you find yourself in a place you'd never have thought possible.

There's no doubt that, as women, we face tough, unique challenges because of our gender. We're endlessly burdened with worries, fears and expectations that men never have to concern themselves with. We're told that we only need to put our energy into certain areas to receive recognition in our lives; at the same time, we're expected to be everything, in every role, to everyone.

It's exhausting. Demoralising. Frustrating and unjust. *We have two choices.*

We can choose to settle for the limiting hand we've been dealt or we can be brave, throw the cards up in the air, and play our own game.

As women, we've been encouraged to find fault with ourselves and to put everyone else's needs and desires before our own. I implore you to **stop**.

I urge you to step forward and claim your rightful

space in the world. To be proud of who you are and the unique contribution you offer.

To free yourself from the dark emotions that haunt and stifle us and to challenge the negative messages you've been given throughout your life – as well as those you create yourself.

Please don't be the woman who plays it small. Please don't be the woman who gives her life to everyone else then wonders who she is when she finds herself alone. Please don't be the woman who gives up hope that there's anything better.

Be the woman you <u>deserve</u> to be. Be the woman the world <u>needs</u> you to be. Stand tall. Learn to love yourself. Support other women.

Show yourself the love, respect and kindness you show to others, and demand that you receive the same.

I can never turn the clock back and pick up the young, broken Katie of yesteryear. I can't tell her that all will be well or that one day she'll be so immensely proud of the person she's strived hard to become.

But I hope I've encouraged you to believe in *your* magnificence and worth. I hope you now realise you're *more* than good enough (and that you always have been).

I hope I've demonstrated that life *always* has the potential to improve, even when it feels like you're in your darkest hour and everything appears bleak and impossible.

I hope that this book will indeed help to **'pick you up'** when you're having a bad day or you're feeling low.

The rest, however, is up to you.

How you move on with your life from here on is entirely in your hands.

I truly hope that you'll choose a kinder, happier and more self-loving path.

'Pick Ups' To Take Away

♥ As women, we've walked the path of self-hatred far too easily and far too often.

♥ We live in an age that makes it easier for us to speak out and share our stories and opinions.

♥ Thanks to the internet, everything we share, indeed everything we talk about, **has the potential to shift us all towards a path of acceptance and self-love.**

♥ Loving ourselves for who we are and for whatever unique contribution we can bring to the world is **<u>not</u> an impossible dream.**

♥ It's not easy for us to love ourselves when we've forever been told we're not good enough. The *only* cure that will make us happier is learning to love who we truly are.

♥ Learning to love ourselves can be a real struggle, but one that's truly worth our effort.

♥ We must stop seeing women loving themselves as a bad thing and start seeing <u>**it as the only thing we should aim for!**</u>

♥ Boosting the love you have for yourself is very much a personal thing and, at times, it won't be easy. But don't give up, because *any* work you do on yourself, in this area, will only help *change your life for the better.*

♥ Learning to love our bodies is one of the biggest challenges we may have. However, there are things we can do to improve and maintain a healthier and more positive body image.

♥ Stop trying to be the 'ideal size' and instead focus your attention on creating a fuller, happier life. This will bring you much more happiness than the weighing scales ever will.

♥ We have two choices: we can choose to settle for the limiting hand we've been dealt, or we can be brave, throw those cards in the air and play our own game.

♥ Step forward and claim your rightful place in the world. Be proud of who you are, what you offer, and what makes you unique.

♥ Show yourself the love, respect and kindness you show to others, and expect and demand that you receive the same.

♥ **Be the woman you deserve to be...the woman that the world *needs* you to be.**

Dear reader,

I've always dreamt that one day there would be a book with my name on it, and now here we are—you're holding my work in your hands! Thank you so much for allowing me into your life *and* your head-space. It's an honour.

My intention when writing this book was always to help women feel better about themselves. If you've enjoyed this book or feel in any way happier or more positive about yourself as a result, I would truly love to hear about it. You can contact me directly at katie@poutinginheels.com.

My hope is that this book speaks to as many women as possible. But to make this happen, I need your help. If you could spare a few minutes to write a review on a retailer's site, to share your thoughts on social media, or even pass this book to a friend you think may benefit from reading it, I will forever be grateful. Thank you so, so much.

Katie x

About the author

Katie Portman is an award-winning blogger, freelance writer and copywriter. Originally from Lancashire, she now lives in Yorkshire with her husband and two children.

Katie has been an Essentials magazine cover girl and was once awarded the title of 'best pout in Yorkshire'. She describes herself as an ordinary woman doing her best to create an extraordinary life. Her lifestyle and parenting blog, Pouting In Heels, has scooped Katie two awards in the seven years she's been blogging. It was created to inspire women to be happier, to do better, and to reach higher. This is her first book.

poutinginheels.com

Praise for Katie's work

'Katie is a one-woman whirlwind of real-life inspiration and sassy northern soul! And she's certainly not one to hold back her opinion! Pouting In Heels is such a happy place, a blog I've followed for years.'

'From the minute you read Pouting In Heels, you want to be Katie's friend, and you also want to celebrate women everywhere.'

'The word I choose to describe Katie is 'frank'. Not in a blunt, outlandish sort of way, but with a sincere openness to talk about subjects we sometimes don't want to approach; her openness is so refreshing. Reading her blog is honestly like having a conversation with a close friend. Who doesn't want that?'

'Katie writes really well, and her posts are the kind of thing you can really get lost in—and ones that you'll remember long after you read them.'

'Each of us gets down on ourselves from time to time, and we can be our own worst critic. Katie writes some fantastic pep talks that help put the spring back in her readers' steps.'

Acknowledgements

This book would not have been possible without the love, support and encouragement of so many people.

To Diane, my publisher, for encouraging me to share my voice with the world in a book! Thank you for your expertise, support and patience and for helping me make a childhood dream come true. I will always be grateful for the belief you've shown in me.

To Charlotte, for doing *the* most beautiful job of illustrating the cover. Shine on, my fellow creative friend.

To my loyal and supportive Pouting In Heels' followers. I am still continually astounded and humbled that so many of you still care about what I have to say. Thank you for making my online world a warm, friendly and wonderful place to be, and for making this career of mine possible.

To my blogger friends, for sharing their voices and stories with the world. Thank you for the continuous inspiration. I'm forever in awe of the talent that exists in our community.

To Mum, for everything you've ever done for me, but also for introducing me at the youngest of ages to the magical world of books. Who knew all those years ago, when you were teaching me how to read and write before I went to school, that one day I would write a book?! It *all* started there. I love you.

To Dad and Lainey, for everything you've ever done for me, but also for helping me to see the world as a hive of positivity and possibility when I was stuck in a very dark place. Your understanding and support helped to change everything. I love you.

To Sal, for being my rock and the best friend I could ever have wished for in a sister. I'm so proud of you for all you've achieved and eternally grateful to have you in my life. I love you.

To Ad, Sylve and Eve—you three, together with Sal, have been a constant source of love, happiness and laughter throughout my life. How lucky we all are to have each other, and our own children now. I love you all. Beavers forever!

To Janine, for always offering a helping hand and for welcoming me so warmly into the family. I couldn't have wished for a kinder or more supportive mother-in-law.

To my Aunty Marg, for being one of the kindest and most courageous women I've ever met. Australia is lucky to have you!

To my nieces and nephews, for bringing much happiness to so many, including me. Never underestimate the power you have to change the world! I love you all.

To Pat, for your friendship and guidance. Thank you for teaching me the journalism ropes and for being a constant source of inspiration. You'll always be part of my family.

To Mayah, thank you for believing in me, and for being kindness personified on more than one occasion.

To my good friends Alison, Ceri, Christina, Helen, Laura, Lisa, Nikki and Sam, and my sister-in-law Laura P—for all the good times, the laughter, the support and the advice. I hope you all know how wonderful you are.

And finally…

To Jamie, my love and best friend, for showing me nothing but unconditional love from the first day we met and for being the biggest source of encouragement and support in my adult life. I couldn't have wished for a more magnificent man to spend my life with and build a family. I love you more than you know.

To Elsie and Leo, for being my proudest achievements and the greatest gifts I have *ever* received. From the tops of your heads to the tips of your toes, every part of you is simply magical to me. Never forget the power that lies within you. I will love you forever and ever and ever.

And to my grandparents, Peggy and Bill and Robert and Mary—no longer of this world but whose presence is forever felt—for the legacy you left that lives on within us all, and for the love and support you endlessly showered me with. I hope I have made you all as proud as you made me. I miss and love you every single day.

THANK YOU!

♥